ALIENS VS PREDATOR REQUIEM

INSIDE THE MONSTER SHOP

ALEC GILLIS and TOM WOODRUFF, JR.

with CHRIS AYERS

designstudio | PRESS

DEDICATION

Websites, message boards, and blogs have all turned fans into critics and opinions into facts. We've had our share of praise and criticism, and still the Alien and the Predator continue to thrill. With this book we seek to show you the people and the art behind the process, answer the question of how it was done, and if we're lucky, inspire the next generation of artists and film-makers. This one is for the fans...

Fox Licensing: Debbie Olshan

Copy Editor: Kate Soto

Book design: Chris Ayers

Photography: James Dittiger, Mark Hanauer, Tom Woodruff Jr., Yuri Everson, Eric Mises-Rosenfeld, Joshua Cordes, Chris Ayers, and Matt Sheehan

Published by Design Studio Press
8577 Higuera Street
Culver City, CA 90232
http://www.designstudiopress.com
E-mail: Info@designstudiopress.com

10 9 8 7 6 5 4 3 2 1

Printed in China
First Edition, December 2007

Library of Congress Control Number:
2007936946

Paperback ISBN-10: 193349255-4
            ISBN-13: 978-193349255-1
Hardcover ISBN-10: 193349252-X
            ISBN-13: 978-193349252-0

contents

Following up the success of *Alien vs. Predator* with a sequel involved far more than just the reprise it may seem at first glance. Given the Strause Brothers' direction and Fox's support of more hard-edged and graphic content, there was a need to develop more horrific visions for the screen. In addition, the Predator character was to be entirely reconceived as a stunning contrast to what had gone before. Likewise, the Alien underwent some structural changes; and there was the PredAlien— the creature that bridges the worlds of the Predator and the Alien. And it all had to be done in record time—four months!

As pre-production and build times become more challenging, it has become more of a necessity to have the right people in place, ready to answer that challenge. Once again we open our creature effects world to present a glimpse of the artists and technicians who have honed the skills that go into creating these legendary movie monsters and the expertise to follow through as creative professionals. Without the dedication of the talented artists featured on these pages, as well as the ones who missed "picture days" when our photos were shot, the challenge would go unanswered. The following pages are dense with images that say far more about the process than the written word can, and with more depth and impact.

But words will have to suffice to express our continued appreciation for the support of Twentieth Century Fox in this ongoing story. Tom Rothman and Hutch Parker set the machine in motion and allowed us the freedom to conceive and create the creatures

integral to their project. We were extremely fortunate to have the enthusiasm and dedication of Alex Young in developing the project in its entirety. Mike Hendrickson was also instrumental in keeping the process moving forward in a positive and productive manner. Jon Davis again provided a valuable resource as we delved into his Predator world and drew from it while creating the new Predator and the Pred-Alien. Paul Deason joined the front from the very beginning, and he and Warren Carr entered the trenches as soon as we hit the ground running in Vancouver. Both were strong allies in keeping us pointed in the right direction, juggling our needs with those of the entire production, and seeing that we all made it to the finish line with a film to show for all the hard work.

Thank you to Shane Salerno for bringing these creatures into our world and for devising the story that would pit them against each other in a hugely satisfying way.

Yet all of the art and the support and the momentum would have had nothing to serve if not for the Strause Brothers. As directors, this team brings a unique visual style to the project, matched only by their love of the genre. With a strong hand in digital effects and amazing CGI accomplishments, they still see the need for real and tactile on-set creature effects to accomplish what is needed of the Aliens, the Predators, and the PredAlien. And for guys that often go without much sleep, they were remarkably coherent through the many long days and long nights on the front line...

When you're making your feature directorial debut in the combined eighth installment of two of the greatest monster movies in cinematic history, things can get a little overwhelming. Even though Greg and I have been fans of the *Alien* movies since before it was probably healthy for us to be watching them, it was great to work with two guys who have been involved for the long haul. Although we're sure Tom and Alec both broke out in a cold sweat when they heard the directors were also visual effects supervisors who own their own VFX facility, they quickly learned how much we love doing "real" effects. No CG in the world can recreate the horror on an actress's face when an Alien's lips are quivering inches away from it, or the shock and awe of a Predator with his lasers focused, hulking above an actor. This is what making these kinds of movies is all about.

On our first visit to ADI we knew it was going to be tough to play it cool, so we decided to just geek out and get it over with. Seeing everything from the Runner to the Original Queen was really inspiring, and it dawned on us how much fun it was going to be to shoot this film. This was our chance to add to the legacy that our idols have created.

The design process was intense and exciting, and Alec, Tom, and their team of talented artists really stepped up to the plate. We were adamant about creating a new, unique Predator with a physique and features that reflected the original films—and the Wolf achieved that in spades.

For our Alien, we also wanted to contribute something different while staying within the existing designs. We've always loved how the ridged heads in *Aliens* seem to blend in with the environment of the hive. You never know if you are looking at a tail, head, or arm—just that it is moving and it is coming to kill you. So that very first day at ADI we all agreed that the ridged heads should reappear in the new film, and they did with a vengeance. The new head has been compared to a chainsaw, and we would have to agree.

We knew from the beginning the most challenging and undoubtedly the most controversial design of the film was going to be the PredAlien. Everyone seems to have their own ideas about this one, but we all agreed that it had to be a big, bad-ass Alien with enough Predator characteristics to make it new and exciting. Alec and Tom came to us with spine-like dreads, and we just went wild for them. The concept designs were awesome; really each one could have been the star of a new franchise. But we kept pushing until we'd found the right balance in what we affectionately call Chet. (After the jerky older brother in *Weird Science*. I'm still not sure if it makes sense but somehow it stuck.)

On set, well... let's just say Tom *is* the Alien; the Alien *is* Tom. He had to pull double-duty this time around playing both the Alien and the PredAlien, and it was amazing to see him bring to life two different creatures with nothing more than his physical prowess. And let us not forget Alec, who is the beauty to Tom's beast. Basically he just sits there and looks cool with his awesome anchorman 'fro, and he helps keep things loose on set. In all seriousness, though, Alec brings an enormous attention to detail, along with the mind of a true storyteller, to the proceedings. He was an invaluable asset to our production.

Ian Whyte made his triumphant return to the role of the Predator. Tom and Alec told us he was the real deal, and he certainly didn't disappoint. Ian showed up in great shape and really played the Wolf as the Dirty Harry of Predators: tough, no-nonsense, and aggressive... the destroyer of Aliens.

The entire ADI crew was a constant boon for us, both in getting this ambitious film done on an extremely tight schedule, and in lightening things up. Even though, historically, practical effects and visual effects are on the opposite sides of the spectrum, it turns out we both share an affinity for inappropriate humor, gory movies, and delicious steak. If that's not friendship we don't know what is.

—*Colin & Greg Strause*

back for more

We've got the kind of job that people make faces at. That's not meant in a negative way; it's just that when people ask the cocktail party question "What line of work are you in?" there's usually an expression of perplexity or outright confusion that follows the answer: "I make monsters." Most people just don't think of monster making as an actual career. If you're reading this you're probably an exception because, as a fan, you've read articles or watched the supplemental material on DVDs featuring this kind of work. To most people, however, what we do at ADI is a mysterious process. Rather than give detailed descriptions of how movie monsters are made, we usually simply state that we make the Alien and the Predator, and the look of confusion disappears. The Alien and the Predator occupy more of the public "mindshare" than any other creatures we've created. For almost 20 years these characters have tenaciously chomped down on the public's imagination and have refused to let go. The list of talent associated with these films is impressive: Ridley Scott, H.R Giger, Dan O'Bannon, Ron Schusett, Walter Hill, James Cameron, Gail Hurd, Sigourney Weaver, David Fincher, Alex Thompson, Jean-Pierre Jeunet, Darius Kondji, Paul Anderson, John McTiernan, Arnold Schwarzenegger, Joel Silver, Stan Winston, and the list goes on, from top physical effects and visual effects artists to the best production designers and composers. These two man-eating space monsters have had the best support crew the movies could muster.

So how'd we get involved? Well, having served time on all but one of the *Alien* films and having created the creatures for *AVP*, you might say we know the drill. Despite our familiarity with the territory we were still thrilled when Alex Young and John Davis sent us the script for *AVP2*. Along with it came the great opportunity to explore some new ground—a new Predator and the ultimate hybrid, the PredAlien. Added to that were the Strause Brothers, Greg and Colin, whose excellent work in commercials and videos made them top contenders

Opposite: One of the galaxy's most feared sportsmen, the silent and stealthy Predator.

Below: Co-Director Colin Strause likes what he sees while reviewing PredAlien maquettes at an early meeting in the ADI display room.

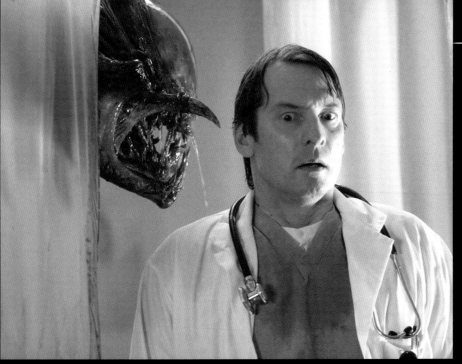

Above: When the PredAlien comes in for a check-up, this unfortunate doctor (Adrian Hough) will be checking out.

as directors. The fact that they are also the creative visionaries behind Hydraulx, one of Hollywood's best digital effects companies, cinched the job for them.

From the beginning the atmosphere was one of teamwork. We all knew that the lean-and-mean approach of the film meant we had to work to all of our strengths and experience. To that end, the filmmakers asked early on for our input on the possible biology of this new life form, the PredAlien. Although the writer, Shane Salerno, and Fox exec Alex Young had no shortage of ideas themselves, it was nice to be included in the process at such an early stage. Here are some of the "Xenobiology Notes" we came up with.

1) The PredAlien capitalizes on the strengths of the genetic roots of its combined heritage:

Alien
Acid blood
Hard exoskeleton
Fast and powerful
Lethal tail
Striking inner mouth
Inter-species hive communication

Predator
Tremendous strength
Warrior/hunter mentality
Fast and powerful
Tool-user (weapons)

2) PredAlien Reproduction

a)
- PredAlien uses tail to inject an acid that carries its own DNA material into a host organism, creating an acid-filled amniotic sac.
- Host organism's birth sac immediately swells and splits.
- New hybrid PredAlien emerges from frothy, bloody afterbirth, five-feet tall, and growing more rapidly than an Alien counterpart would.
- PredAlien exhibits characteristics of the host organism from which it develops.
- The entire reproduction, from injection to emergence, takes place before our eyes.
- The new PredAlien consumes the afterbirth material...its first meal.
- Its rapid rate of growth means it needs to feed.

b)
- PredAlien first "impregnates" an animal—a bull or a large dog.
- We see only the results of the process this first time (in the form of an acid-eaten hole in the ground with the sloughed-off skin of a bull nearby).
- A five-foot tall newborn quadruped creature attacks and is dispatched.
- Later, we'll see the detail of the impregnation and swelling of a human host.

3) The PredAlien DNA that attacks the host cells is a cancerous growth model.

4) We also imagined what might happen if some teenagers ever got hold of some of the Predator weapons.

Interaction with Locals
- Wise-ass kids find the crashed Predator ship, still in cloaked mode.
- They are amazed by the invisible ship.
- They find their way to an opening and enter; once inside, the interior ship is in full view.
- They find remnants of a collection of species held in stasis.
- They perhaps uncover some aspects of the escaped PredAlien.
- Perhaps they unwittingly help or allow the PredAlien to escape.
- They discover the armory, then find and take armor, helmets, and weapons.
- They examine their loot later in the car.
- Tension builds as they point business end of retracted Wrist Blades toward their own faces.
- Suspense rises as they recognize the Shoulder Cannon to be a gun of some sort.
- They blast a cow into pieces with it as they drive by.
- The force of the blast nearly sends the car out of control.
- The kids are confused by the misleadingly innocent-looking Shuriken and Spear.
- They hit the button, and the Spear immediately deploys.
- One end shoots up, piercing the roof of the car.
- The other end shoots through the kid's leg and the floor of the car.
- The tip digs into the asphalt at 60 mph, tearing his leg to pieces.

As you can see, many ideas splatter on the ground after being thrown from the speeding train of production, but the process of conceptualizing is invaluable. It allows everyone to plant boundary markers around the movie, to help establish a perimeter of thought, and perhaps most importantly, to get to know each other creatively. Once you've got the team comfortable with each other the fun can start. That's where the back and forth of design begins, with the actual building of the creatures hot on its heels!

In the case of *AVP2* we were fortunate to have directors who loved the characters, studio execs who really cared about the movie and its fan base, and a terrific crew at ADI and in Canada who creatively invested themselves in the project. If we all have done our jobs, the Alien and the Predator just might keep sinking their teeth into the audience's imagination for years to come.

Left: After an Earthly splashdown, the Wolf emerges!

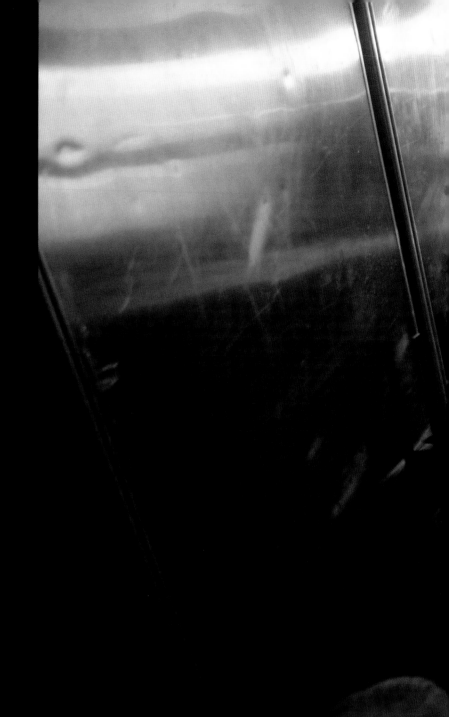

bring on the misery!

A liens vs. Predator: Requiem was to be shot entirely on location in Vancouver, British Columbia, which meant we would be giving up the picturesque location of the first film's Prague location in favor of a much closer and more convenient locale. The 50-day shoot began on September 25 and wrapped December 8, 2006.

What made this shoot unusual was that for the first time Aliens would be seen on the streets of small-town America—in the sewers, amid the grating of an outdoor power plant, and on the rooftops. The directors, Greg and Colin Strause, would also be staging most of the exterior action at night in the rain. The shorter days of winter would provide longer nights for the exterior shoots, and a number of crane-rigged rain pipes would ensure there be no shortage of torrential rain!

In the past, our Aliens have always played within the controlled environments of the studio stage. But this time, outdoor shooting in varied locations for both the Predator and Aliens would mean the new challenge of presenting these characters at their sci-fi best.

The burden of moving our entire crew and creature inventory every few nights while supplying Predators and Aliens for two separate shooting units became a major effort of manpower coordination for our small crew. On top of this, we had another crew of artists working a day shift to keep up with repairs of the night's shooting. They were also working to complete items on our build list that couldn't be finished before relocating to Vancouver. And with the prospect of a harsh winter and night exteriors shot in the rain without the benefit of any kind of thermal solution for the suit performers, we soon found ourselves in middle of the most physically challenging shoot of our career.

Previous spread: The *AVP2* crew prepares to shoot a scene in the kitchen of a diner.

Opposite: Steve Frakes is *just* tall enough to make a last-minute adjustment to the Predator before the cameras roll.

Below: Frank Meschkuleit, Paul Hooson, Adam Behr, and Garth Winkless snap an Alien into his suit on location in Vancouver, British Colombia.

17

Much as it appeared on our final contract, here is a listing of what had to be designed and built:

AVP-style Predators
Living Predator x 1
Dead Predator bodies—damaged by PredAlien x 2
Refurbish "Scar" Predator from *AVP* for Chestbursting opening
Build:
    Body suit/hands/feet x 2
    Stunt head with helmet x 2
    Armor (configuration TBD) x 2
    "Scar" dummy refurbish x 1

AVP-style Hybrid Chestbursters
Quick flashes of coverage as it bursts—lots of blood
Build:
    Refurbish x 1
    Rigid burst-through with sloughing skin

New Predator
"The Wolf" character
New custom Animatronic character
Heavy body scarring—battle damage
Armor bid separately below
Build:
    Custom sculpture and molds
    Body suit/hands/feet x 6
    Animatronic head with exposed face x 2
    Stunt head with exposed face x 2
    Stunt head for helmet (no exposed face) x 2
    Slashed-leg appliances
    Acid-burn body appliances
    Slashed left-arm appliances
    Abdomen stabbed by the PredAlien claws appliance
    Articulated dummy

Predator Armor and Weapons
New custom armor for "The Wolf" character
"Hero" armor indicates rigid finish for detailed coverage.
"Stunt" armor indicates similar look to hero pieces, but resilient for all work.
"Practical" weapons and tools indicate working lights, moving covers, etc.
"Stunt" weapons and tools indicate non-functioning resilient pieces for all work.
All electronic components will be built and shielded to work in wet, rainy conditions.
Build:
    Custom sculpture and molds
    Hero armor x 1
    Stunt armor x 4
    Hero helmet x 2
    Hero helmet with damaged laser sight x 2
    Hero helmet with full damage x 2
    Double Wrist Blades—practical x 1
    Double Wrist Blades—stunt x 2
    Additional blades
    Arm cladding deployed—stunt x 2
    Wrist Computer—practical x 1
    Wrist Computer—stunt (with lights) x 2
    Slashed Wrist Computer x 2
    Closed Spear x 2
    Extended Spear x 4 (one rigged to travel as

Above: The fully equipped Predator begins his hunt.

    thrown Spear on guide line)
    Shuriken—closed x 4
    Shuriken—closed discs to pack into case x 4
    Shuriken—open hero x 2
    Shuriken—open stunt x 4
    Bullwhip—x 3
    Hero Claymore mines x 2
    Stunt Claymore mines (with lights) x 8
    Cleaner Case—practical x 1 (incorporates new bomb)
    Cleaner Case—closed stunt x 1
    Tracking Syringe—practical x 1
    Bandolier x 4
    Vials of Dissolving Liquid—practical x 2
    Vials of Dissolving Liquid—stunt x 2
    New gun sculpture and molds
    Dual Shoulder Cannons—practical x 2
    Dual Shoulder Cannons—stunt x 2
    Battle-damaged Shoulder Cannon x 1
    Handheld Shoulder Cannon—practical x 2
    Handheld Shoulder Cannon—stunt x 2
    Backpack with deploying dual Shoulder Cannons—practical x 1
    Backpack with Med Kit—practical x 1
    Backpack with closed Med Kit and Cannons already deployed—stunt x 2
    Additional Med Kit instruments—TBD
    Additional cleaner case instruments—TBD

Warrior Aliens
New design of head and neck
Reuse of existing library of molds
Component pieces for Alien injuries, maims, and kills
(Final assembly of component pieces to occur on set—not covered in this budget.)

Build:
Harness/rigging wirework R&D
Motion rising base
Revised head and neck—sculpture through molding
Body suits/hands/feet x 12
Animatronic heads x 4
Stunt heads x 9
Animatronic head with working inner mouth x 1
Refurbish mechanical insert tail x 1
Floppy tail x 8
Self-supporting tail x 3
Articulated stunt dummy x 2
Kills/maim component pieces
Alien blood effects

Facehuggers
Refurbish existing Hero Animatronic
Reuse of existing library of molds
> **Build:**
> Refurbish Animatronic (add probe) x 1
> Running puppet on pull line x 2
> Hand puppet version x 2
> Stunt puppet x 6
> "Skeletal" version x 2

Chestbursters
Reuse of existing library of molds
> **Build:**
> "Pop-out" Chestbursters x 1
> Articulated Chestbursters x 1
> Floppy Chestbursters rod puppets x 4

PredAlien
New custom Animatronic character
Combine elements of Alien Warrior and Predator
> **Build:**
> Growth-stage puppet x 1
> Shed skin x 2
> Animatronic adult hero x 1

Adult body suits/hand/feet x 4
Animatronic head x 2
Stunt head x 2
Insert gloved hands pair x 2
Articulated insert arm extension pair x 2
Floppy tail x 2
Self-supporting tail x 2
Predator blades stabbed in neck
Predator melted left arm into torso or head—reveal x 1
PredAlien blood effects

Human Effects
Design to allow minimal exposure suitable for PG-13 rating
Extended coverage of same build can provide material suitable for R rating
> **Build:**
> Buddy's dismembered hand x 1
> Harry blown-open chest appliance x 1
> Additional homeless chest appliance x 1
> Ray skinned body with skinning effect x 1
> Carrie blown-out stomach appliance
> Karl blow-up back of head x 3
> Dale acid-burn skin appliance x 1
> Pregnant Sue's bulging, rippling body appliance x 1
> Pregnant Sue's body bursts open x 3
> Blown-open pregnant appliances x 3
> Female dummy bodies x 4
> ER Doctor profile head strike x 1
> Blood effects

Below: Co-Director Greg Strause, Alec Gillis, Tom Woodruff, Jr. (in Alien suit), Dave Penikas, Frank Meschkuleit, and Adam Behr prepare for a complex shot involving an Alien Warrior and two Facehuggers (one a hand puppet and one operated via radio control). The large black tube in the background was used to pump smoke into the shot for added atmosphere.

Left: ADI crew members attempt to stay warm and keep their radio control units dry while puppeteering the Animatronic elements of both the Predator and PredAlien during the climactic rooftop battle.

The challenges of the schedule were going to be daunting, as we couldn't commence the project until Fox was ready to launch into official pre-production in mid-June. With a start date of mid-September, this would allow only three months of full attention in the shop to design and produce most of that list above, including a new Predator and, demanding most of our design focus, the long-anticipated PredAlien!

Luckily for us all, we are veterans of the drill. Pre-production times have been shrinking while the audience is growing more discerning and demanding. It is becoming more and more of a challenge to achieve the artistic success necessary to satisfy the audience, but if anyone were going to pull off such an ambitious project, it would be ADI.

The On-Set Crew

Despite the proximity of Vancouver, our department was limited in the number of puppeteers we could import for the shoot. In the past, bringing an L.A.–based crew was not as much of an issue, and we could staff the puppeteers and technicians with whom we've built a solid resume. But film productions shot outside the U.S. often offer government incentives that are tied to how many crew members are locals—ironically in many cases, we, the creators of the creatures, have been considered a "bad spend." Working with production, we arrived at a number of U.S crew members that worked best for our efficiency and the studio's budget. Although we were creating the stars of the movie, resources would be tight!

While we fully expected shooting demands to require up to 20 puppeteers, only eight of them would be drawn from our shop, comprised of the artists and technicians who actually designed and built the complicated Animatronics. We would once again be assembling a very experienced puppeteer cast, all talented artists who have worked with us on many shows over the years, including *AVP*. They were Yuri Everson, Garth Winkless, Dave Penikas, Marc Irvin, Hiroshi Ikeuchi, and Steve Frakes.

In our Vancouver workshop there were still some pieces to be built, notably the skinned bodies of Deputy Ray and two Predators. Rounding out our crew was a handful of the top makeup and creature effects artists in Canada. The team was headed by Mike Fields, who fit in well with the ADI crew as he too was a jack-of-all-trades, comfortable hopping from suit dresser to puppeteer to makeup artist. Once his on-set duties kicked in, the Creature Workshop Lead went to the very talented Maiko Gomyo, who supervised a terrific crew comprised of J.P. Mass, Gideon Hay, and Charlie

Below: In ADI's temporary Vancouver shop, Mike Fields produces mesentery membranes used to create the spectacularly gory demise of many Aliens.

ADI's on-set crew members must be prepared for anything. As well-planned as a movie shoot can be, the unexpected always seems to happen—whether it be creative brainstorming for a new "must have" shot, last-minute script changes, or the unpredictable Mother Nature herself.

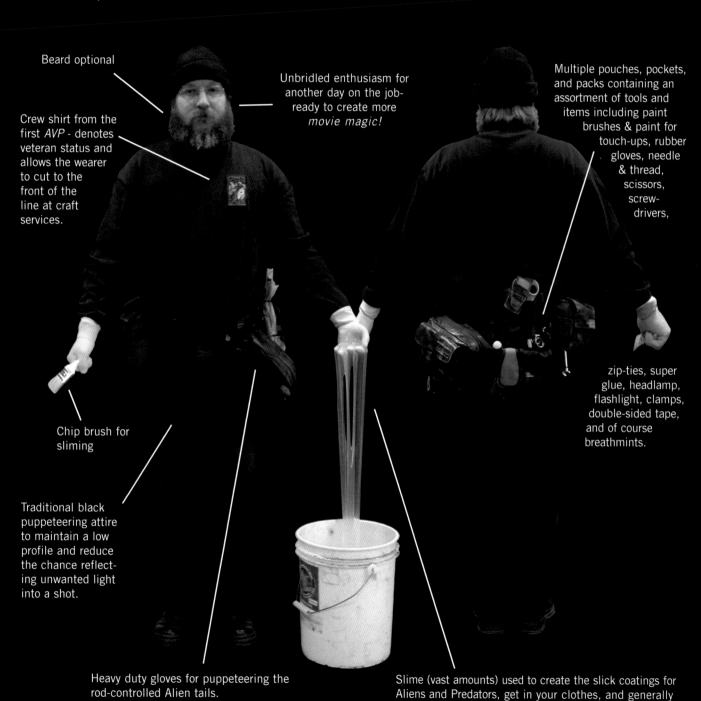

Beard optional

Unbridled enthusiasm for another day on the job-ready to create more *movie magic!*

Crew shirt from the first *AVP* - denotes veteran status and allows the wearer to cut to the front of the line at craft services.

Multiple pouches, pockets, and packs containing an assortment of tools and items including paint brushes & paint for touch-ups, rubber gloves, needle & thread, scissors, screw-drivers,

Chip brush for sliming

zip-ties, super glue, headlamp, flashlight, clamps, double-sided tape, and of course breathmints.

Traditional black puppeteering attire to maintain a low profile and reduce the chance reflecting unwanted light into a shot.

Heavy duty gloves for puppeteering the rod-controlled Alien tails.

Slime (vast amounts) used to create the slick coatings for Aliens and Predators, get in your clothes, and generally make a mess of things.

Above: In *AVP2* we find out that things *do* go bump in the night.
Left: Frank Meschkuleit catches oozing Alien innards after the Predator demonstrates his skill with a bullwhip.
Opposite: Aliens show up for a showdown at Big Dean's Sporting Goods. "Clean up in aisle five!"

Sewer Entrance

The first day of shooting was a foreshadowing of things to come. The action called for an Alien to follow two Facehuggers into a sewer entrance. It was an actual location, which was fortunately a storm sewer, not a concrete river of human waste. *Un*fortunately, it was cramped and difficult to set up our effects and hide puppeteers. With most of the crew crammed in there, we were longing for the wide-open spaces of a phone booth. Tom was outside in an Alien suit, draped in a shedding skin. Inside was our Running Facehugger, which was rigged on wires and operated by Alec and Dave Penikas. Puppeteers Frank Meschkuleit and Yuri Everson were operating a hand-puppet Facehugger that was crawling into the sewer from above. It was an ambitious and jam-packed first day—and there would be many more like it!

Molly's Backyard

It was still relatively early in the schedule for this night shoot and the weather hadn't become much of an issue—yet. This was also one of the few exteriors in which the creatures did not work under the non-stop rain machines.

It was, however, a real neighborhood, complete with families and kids on the street late into the night. Our truck was set up on one of the side streets away from the action, but it was hard to be inconspicuous when the only way in and out of the truck was the full-size roll-up door that revealed a rack of Alien and Predator costumes, heads, and armor when open. It wasn't long before a squadron of locals was camped out at the back of the truck, hoping to catch another glimpse. Production provided an assistant to guard the truck.

Above: Allison Chretien holds a Facehugger in place while ... Fields attaches it to actor Kurt Max Runte (Buddy).

During a break in shooting, Greg took us into the backyard of the Molly's house, while Colin spotted a good location to reveal the Alien from the upstairs window, using a real night-vision scope. Greg pointed out the steep fall-off a few feet into the woods, next to the path where the Alien would be performing, virtually blind. We blocked out a simple move and headed to the truck to suit up the Alien. Fully dressed except for the head, Tom was shrouded in blankets and hurried into a van to be driven through the crowd to the house. As soon as the van stopped, he ran along the side of the house to get into the backyard, away from the lights and the spectators and into view of the night-vision camera.

Once in frame, a surprising discovery was made: Aliens don't look so good in night-vision! Without the benefit of the viscous coating of slime to reflect highlights of the sculptural details, the costume simply looked like a rubber suit. Plus, in the wide-angle coverage needed for the shot, it was impossible to hide Tom's legs and human proportions. A different path for the action was chosen, one that ran through the middle of a rose garden we had been asked to steer clear of, and which had a steep drop off on the other side! The head was put on, rendering Tom virtually blind in the dark.

As it turns out, the Alien exoskeleton was no match for rose thorns, which stabbed their way into Tom's arms and legs. At least the pain provided confirmation

...e: A Chest-
...er puppet was
...ly inflated to
...rough a tear-
...shirt. Faintly
...e is the wire
...to assist the
...et's deployment.

...: Dressed to
perfection, a
...burster
...ges from
...y's torso.

that Tom was not about to plunge over the edge of the drop, even if a few bushes became collateral damage. The additional brush served its purpose of hiding Tom's legs, but in the end not a bush was untouched. It was the first suit-repair job on the movie.

To cap off the night, all our secrecy was for naught, as a neighborhood kid posted a report on an *Alien* website describing the entire shoot.

Into the Woods

Poor Buddy and Sam. They're the father and son who run afoul of Facehuggers while out hunting. The location for their demise was a beautiful forest outside Vancouver that looked like something from Earth's distant primordial past. As we from L.A. marveled at its uniqueness, a local crew person told us that *The X-Files* shot there "a million times." The moss was actually killing the trees from which it eerily hung, another crew member told us. All right, so it was overused and diseased, but the trees made a great backdrop for an Alien attack that would see Buddy shoot a Facehugger, get his arm melted off, and have a Chestburster tear through his ribcage. This short scene would require Facehugger hand puppets, squibbed Floppy Facehuggers, the burst-through Chestbursters, the Hero Animatronic Chestbursters, Buddy's melted arm appliance and severed arm, and two burst-open chest wounds. Hunting isn't cool.

Later in the story, the Predator dissolves all signs of an Alien encounter. Bubbly, gooey mats in the outline of the Facehuggers and their human victims were created so that the digital artists at Hydraulx could provide a melting effect. These woods would also see one of the more gruesome effects in the film: Deputy Ray's skinned body, hanging bloody and lifeless—a reminder not to sneak up on a Predator. Using component pieces made at ADI in L.A., our Vancouver crew assembled, painted, and finished the corpse to disgusting perfection.

Above: Alec Gillis spritzes the skinned body of Deputy Ray to keep him slick for another take.

Below: The flayed dummy, fabricated over a replica skeleton by the ADI Vancouver crew, receives a coat of paint from Maiko Gomyo.

The Predator Debut

The first use of the new Predator suit was also the character's first appearance in the film. It was a "magic hour" shot of the Predator emerging from a lake, decloaking, and wading ashore. The sticky mud on the bottom of the lake required a team of divers to place a wood ramp under water, insuring an effortless introduction of the character. All went well until rehearsal of the Predator's run from the imploding spaceship, when Ian Whyte took a spill in the forest. A quick redesign of the eye lenses by Yuri and Garth and we were ready to shoot. Ultimately, the Predator's emergence from the lake would be re-shot on a green-screen stage, where the lighting could be controlled. "Magic hour" actually only lasts about 15 minutes.

Molly's Bedroom

From the backyard, the Alien makes his move on the humans in the bedroom, and the window doesn't slow him down. The crash-through-the-window stunt was complicated by the narrow clearance and mini blinds. Tom worked with stunt coordinator J.J. Makaro to advise on performance issues and the best way to look like an Alien traveling through a sheet of break-away glass, but it was stuntman Simon Burnett who was charged with pulling off the gag.

With the stunt out of the way, it was Tom's turn to play the Alien killing Molly's Dad. Soon Tom found himself straddling an actor he had met in the hotel elevator just the day before. Sometimes the closest relationships are forged quickly on set.

Below: One of the *AVP2* camera crews catches the action on location in Vancouver.

Above: Pregnant waitress Carrie (Gina Holden) is menaced by Aliens, however it's not them she has to worry about.

Right: After a gruesome encounter with the PredAlien, poor Carrie is not even eating for one anymore.

The Diner

The diner scene was to be an important early glimpse of the PredAlien, intended to show its dominance over warrior Aliens, imply a bizarre new mode of procreation, and raise the stakes for the audience. The only problem was that we still hadn't finished the creature yet. All we had was an Alien Warrior glove modified to look somewhat like the PredAlien's hand for the shot where the Cook's spine is ripped from his body. One of the upsides of working with the Strauses is that, as digital artists, they have confidence in their technology. They had planned to shoot a plate of the cowering actress and composite the PredAlien, which would be shot later against a greenscreen. Part of the fun of that was that Tom got to be onscreen as both an Alien Warrior and the PredAlien at the same time!

The Sewer Battle

For the moment, we were back to shooting days on the interior sewer set at Vancouver Film Studio, but things wouldn't be getting any easier. The sewer set was a highly detailed and believable environment of interconnecting tunnels, complete with three feet of water. Raised walkways along each tunnel allowed access above the surface of the water but quickly became a gauntlet of lights and C-stands. Weeks were spent in this environment either in hip waders or hunched over along the walkways, weaving through the maze of equipment in the dark. Slowly, the crew shed our zombie-like state as we all adjusted to the day schedule.

On screen, the images of both the Predator and Alien in the murky waters were eerily striking, as the new watery environment provided opportunities for both hunter and prey to disappear from view. It was a visual theme that would resonate throughout the rest of the story, as a torrential rainstorm provided the same excitement on the streets above ground.

Composed primarily of foam latex, the body suits of the creatures worked effectively as sponges, quickly taking on extra water weight as soon as they slipped into the sewers. While somewhat neutrally buoyant, they could become restrictive enough to make it difficult to regain footing quickly if a performer were to lose balance underwater, so puppeteers kept close watch from off camera.

Once laden with water, the suits also became much more fragile and susceptible to damage. With new story notes coming in during the shoot, the

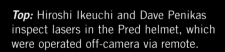

Top: Hiroshi Ikeuchi and Dave Penikas inspect lasers in the Pred helmet, which were operated off-camera via remote.

Above: Hip-deep in water on the sewer set, Jeny Cassady attends to an Alien.

Right: Ian Whyte tosses an Alien stunt performer onto a padded mat during the sewer battle.

sewer sequence was expanded, and even more action was devised, including a centerpiece battle between the Predator, three Aliens, and the PredAlien! It was impossible to develop a more water-resistant approach to suit building overnight, and the extensive rehearsals soon saw body suits of both Alien and Predator falling victim to the strains of stunt fights in the water. With our minimal crew now stretched among the full-time shooting, maintenance of two separate units, and the ongoing build in Canada, Sandi Blackie and her wardrobe department came to the rescue with additional crew to help stay on top of the drying and repairing of suits that lasted all day and all night.

Above: A homeless man (Lloyd Berry) struggles for his life opposite a frisky eight-legged co-star.

Left: Combining features of both the Alien and Predator species, the PredAlien possesses great strength, cunning, agility, and ferocity.

Above: Using the crook of a tree as a makeshift ER, the Wolf tends to his wounds.

Below: Steve Frakes gets a bird's-eye view of the action as he puppeteers an Alien tail.

Despite our goal, the pre-production schedule and set construction budget could not support the more radical wirework planned for the practical Aliens, including techniques we developed for the first *AVP*. Stunt coordinator Makaro was, however, able to devise a clever and effective regimen of supporting stunt Aliens and stunt Predators on wires for a sizeable assortment of stunts. Working with Tom on one particular set-up, Makaro worked out a shot that had the Alien-suited performer lowered from the ceiling of one of the dry sewer tunnels as the Predator passes beneath. A second wire spiraled the Alien during the descent to allow a very spider-like unfolding of torso and limbs. A third wire controlled the tail, allowing it to unwind during the climb to complete the illusion.

The sewers see most of the Facehugger action, with an attack on some homeless characters who live under the streets of Gunnison. We were all pleased that our improved Running Facehugger got some use, despite the fact that the sets were cramped and didn't really allow much space for long runs. One of the actors proved particularly adept at acting in reverse, which helped in the leap onto a character's face. We also redesigned our approach to the wire rigging of the Floppy Facehugger so that more could be shot in forward action.

In between set-ups on the sewer set, ADI presented the finished PredAlien stunt suit to the Strause Brothers for the first time. Although not as detailed as the in-progress "hero" suit and Animatronic head, it was nonetheless a first look at the completed creature. Finished hands were not yet ready so a pair of Alien hands was painted to match the paint scheme of the new creature for the presentation. The PredAlien made a successful, if low-keyed, debut. With most of the crew's attention focused on the shooting at hand, few saw the new creature as the Strause Brothers gave their approval to the next generational offspring of the Alien and the Predator.

Our wish of seeing the end to the long weeks of shooting on the sewer set was fulfilled, as we saw the set fall under the Bobcat tractors the very next day. We didn't know that we would soon actually be missing the sewer set for its relative comfort. Be careful what you wish for...

Limb Surgery

After Aliens attack the Wolf in the power plant, he retreats to high ground, in this case an old tree in a cemetery. Here he uses his signature Med Kit to repair a nasty wound in his side. For the wide shot we posed the articulated Med Kit on the limb in front of Ian, dressed as the Predator. As we were starting to drill a screw into the wood, we heard the panicked voice of the woman whose job it was to protect the tree. Before we could roll our eyes and say "only in Canada," it was explained to us that this was a special tree; so old it was in a registry of old trees. After using bailing wire to gently secure the Med Kit, we began to apply the glowing Predator blood that was supposed to have leaked from his wound and down the tree. Enter same panicked woman, Protector of Special

Trees, who needed to know the ingredients of the Pred blood. Deferring to Tony Lazarowich, Lead Special Effects man, we waited while he ran down the list of ingredients. The woman was either a chemistry genius, or overwhelmed by Tony's sheer quantity of syllables, as she allowed us to continue with our wide shot. Fortunately we had the foresight to plan all close-ups to be shot later in a lower, less special tree.

We were now officially on night shoots.

Shootin' Up the Aliens

We had been given the heads-up that the Aliens and the Predator would be working under wet, rainy conditions, but weren't expecting just how severely the weather was to impact us. Waterproofing the Animatronics inside the creature heads turned out to be the easiest part of the job. The relentless rain machines and the cold of the night shoot were going to be the most difficult challenges.

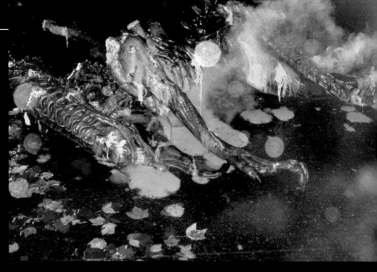

Above: Good ol' fashioned steaming, oozing Alien carnage.

Below: A most-unwanted hitchhiker terrorizes two young Gunnison residents (Meshach Peters and Shareeka Epps).

The wider the shot, the higher in the air the rain towers had to go to hide the cranes that held them above the action. Fed by high-volume water lines, the rain pipes would come on as the cameras started to roll, and even after the cue to "cut" was issued, it would take a few minutes for the pressurized lines to empty, ensuring a lingering downpour. From that height, the weight of the falling rain upon the epoxy shell of the Alien head created a constant noise that hindered communication with Tom inside the suit.

As we moved into winter, the cold nights made the experience even more miserable for all the actors. Warming tents were stationed just out of camera range. Even with the insulation of Costumer Sandi Blackie's low-relief Eco-skin bodysuits worn beneath the costumes, each take would end up being bone-chillingly cold. In many of the Alien and Predator set-ups, it was not often convenient to move the title creatures to the warming tents, as the chilled actors were able to do. In those cases, portable propane heaters were

Above: Mike Fields inspects an Alien before filming begins.

Below: Dave Penikas confirms that an Alien's Animatronic facial features are functioning properly.

Opposite: The Wolf punches his way to the roof of the hospital, intent on ending this battle.

brought to the creature performers between shots to help take the edge of the chill. Many weeks of night shoots were spent in the elements, as the Second Unit First Assistant Director, Ken Shane, would cue the rain machines with a shout of "Bring on the misery!"

The Rooftop

The climactic battle takes place on the rooftop of the hospital as the main characters face the final Alien onslaught and the Predator and the PredAlien finally go head to head! On a few acres of disused Forestry School land, production created the rooftop hospital set, located conveniently at ground level. Since the scene takes place at night, the lack of an actual drop-off didn't matter. It was here that all the action of the Predator's whipping, spearing, and otherwise dispatching of Aliens was filmed. Humans got in on the fun too, shooting up Aliens from the helicopter with machine guns and making good use of the Predator Shoulder Cannon, now in hand-held mode.

As always, Main Unit was in charge of the action, and this scene required more stunt men than any other in the film, many of them being squibbed and pulled on wire ratchets. What would start out as simple stunt shots would often become more complex as the Brothers' creative juices started flowing. "Wouldn't it be cool if there were a hero Alien in the foreground while a stunt Alien got blown away in the background?" Greg or Colin would say, sending Yuri and Garth scurrying off to the truck to start suiting up another performer. Their love of these classic characters compelled the Brothers to make the best use of them. As CG artists themselves, they appreciated the fact that with suit performers, it's not a huge cost to add another monster to the scene. Yet we would soon find out that, unlike with a digital character, inclement weather could create problems for suit performers.

The rooftop set was 45 minutes from Vancouver in a suburb called Surrey. Lovely place, but in late November it's not where you want to hang out in an Alien or Predator suit—in the middle of the night. Covered in slime. In fake rain. While real snow falls. This was the kind of location that made even the hardiest Canadians bundle up in their downiest cold-weather gear. The human cast members had it rough in soaking wet jeans and Pendletons, but at least they could be warmed in between takes by portable heaters and blankets. A creature suit is essentially a full-body sponge that keeps ice-cold water pressed against the performer's skin at all times. Tom had his Eco-skin undersuit to provide some insulation against the cold, but the rain falling from the towers 120 feet up forced near-freezing

Above: It's talons vs. Spear as the PredAlien (Tom Woodruff, Jr.) and Predator (Ian Whyte) face off on the hospital roof.

Above: The alien combatants are given a brief respite from the constant downpour of the rain machines between takes. On-set sources confirm that there was no singin'.

Right: Well… okay. Maybe a little singin'.

water into every nook and cranny (yes, even *that* cranny). At one point, after a particularly long series of takes, Tom was overcome by uncontrollable shaking. Fearing another bout of hypothermia like he experienced on *Alien Resurrection*, Alec stopped the shooting so that Tom could get out of the Alien suit. Production was more than happy to keep their star healthy, especially since Tom was double-cast as the PredAlien! Ian was miserable as well, though his childhood in chilly Newcastle, England, may have helped prepare him for Surrey, British Columbia.

The day after we finished at the rooftop, the entire set was under three feet of snow.

Right: The Predator mask was capable of full eye movement with eye blinks and cheek squints, independent brow articulation, jaw open and close, and double-jointed mandible motion.

Below: Ian Whyte strikes an iconic Predator pose.

Power Trip

AVP2 might be the last movie allowed to shoot at the big power plant outside of Vancouver. We didn't do anything wrong, mind you, but rumor had it that some production before us did, making the management less interested in renting the place out to moviemakers. Luckily, *AVP2*'s Super-Producer John Davis knew that the location was perfect for us, and he made a phone call. Before we knew it, we were shooting Aliens and Predators on the plant's catwalks a dizzying 140 feet off the ground. Ian Whyte was an awesome sight as he stood in full Predator regalia on a metal platform, firing his Shoulder Cannon wildly into the plant's superstructure. He was tethered with a safety line, but it was still a stomach-churning height.

The only classic human kill in the film happens on those catwalks, too. A likeness of our actor was created from a head cast and made into a perfectly detailed replica loaded with an air-powered canister of brains and blood. Timed with the punch of a pneumatic Alien striking tongue, the effect is sickening, even though the brains themselves were bananas from the craft service table.

Above: There is a surge of activity when the Predator encounters Aliens at a massive power station.

Below: Tethered to a safety harness, but with extremely limited vision, a masked Ian Whyte inches into position high among a labyrinth of pipes.

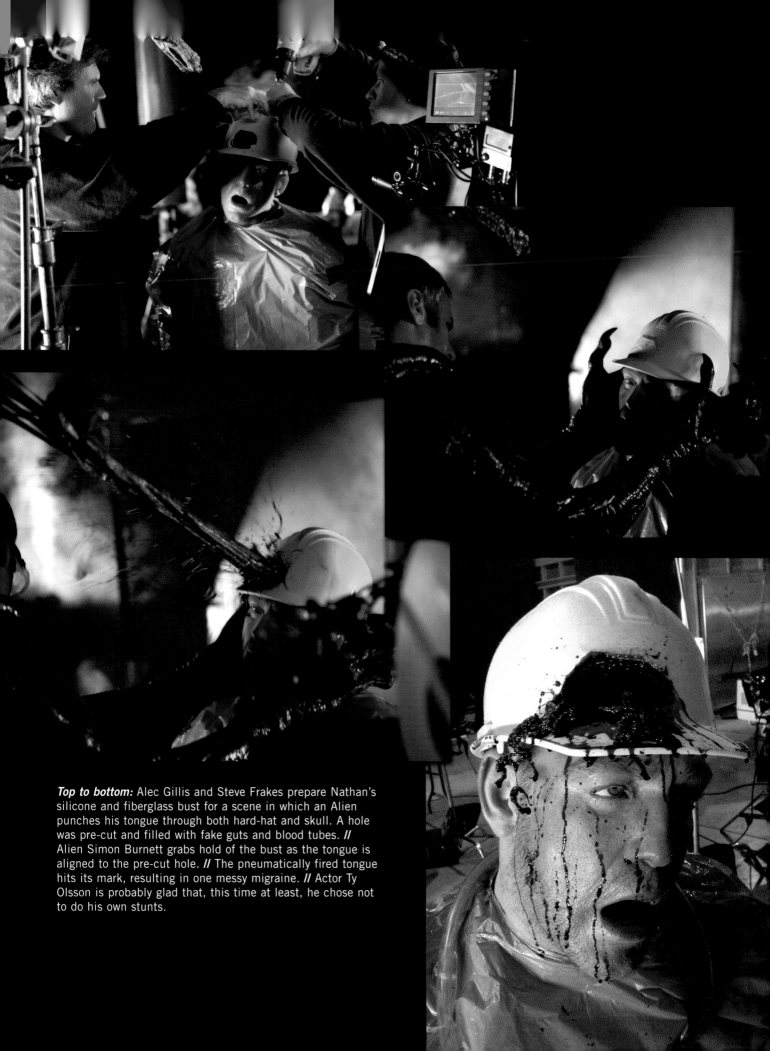

Top to bottom: Alec Gillis and Steve Frakes prepare Nathan's silicone and fiberglass bust for a scene in which an Alien punches his tongue through both hard-hat and skull. A hole was pre-cut and filled with fake guts and blood tubes. **//** Alien Simon Burnett grabs hold of the bust as the tongue is aligned to the pre-cut hole. **//** The pneumatically fired tongue hits its mark, resulting in one messy migraine. **//** Actor Ty Olsson is probably glad that, this time at least, he chose not to do his own stunts.

The Pool

Anybody who has ever taken a swim in a community pool has probably wondered what kind of bugs might be lurking in the water. One Vancouver-area community pool saw some mighty big ones. Shooting at night when the pool was closed allowed us to tow Alien-suited Stunt Coordinator J.J. Makaro through the water, attack teenagers, and spill Alien blood freely. One of the cooler Alien kills in the film has the Wolf spearing an Alien through the back of the head and out of the mouth just as it's about to strike at its human victim! This was an example of "off-the-truck" effects at work. In short order, ADI Mechanical Department Head Dave Penikas was able to modify an existing Hero Animatronic Alien head with a guide tube for the Predator Spear to ride on, while vomiting acid blood, too. Like the Wolf, who uses his vial of Dissolving Liquid to erase traces of the Alien's presence, our crew had to clean up all signs of the night's carnage before the pool opened and the first swimmer arrived the next morning. No horseplay

Opposite page, top: "Swim at Your Own Risk" takes on a whole new meaning when Aliens infest a high school swimming pool.

Opposite page, bottom: The Predator prevents further human carnage as he makes one of his famous Alien kabobs.

Above: Shooting scenes in a Vancouver pool require divers and an aquatic camera platform.

Left: Shooting a close-up of the skewered Alien.

Below: Tom Woodruff, Jr. controls the Predator Spear as it pierces an Alien dummy. At far right, with the radio control box, Hiroshi Ikeuchi puppeteers the Alien's quivering snarl as he takes his final breath.

Right: Tom Woodruff, Jr. prowls through the hospital as the PredAlien, searching for suitable hosts for its offspring.

Below: Mike Fields and Adrian Burnett prep the Animatronic PredAlien puppet for filming.

Bottom: Alec Gillis helps the ADI Animatronics crew line up the PredAlien puppet's extendable mandibles with the face of a victim.

The Hospital

In one of the more twisted scenes in the film, the PredAlien appears at a hospital and stalks the halls, pausing for a moment at the nursery window to look at several plump, helpless, newborn babies. According to Tom, it was one of the strangest experiences of his suit-performing career to find himself dressed as the PredAlien looking through a viewing window in a maternity ward. Actually, the location was a closed-down wing of a mental institution, and we were told to ignore patients from the other wing who might happen to wander through our sets. Perhaps the management was worried that one look at our creatures might drive a person sane.

Clockwise from top left: This visitor most certainly did not bring flowers—the PredAlien prepares to infuse an expectant mother (Victoria Bidewell) with Chestbursters. // Morris Chapdelaine wrangles a pair of Chestburster rod puppets while his creature effects teammates Paul Hooson, Steve Frakes, and Mike Fields attend to other details. // Perhaps now she is having second thoughts about refusing that epidural. // Crew members take precautionary measures to protect both equipment and themselves from ample amounts of flying slime and fake blood before shooting the Chestburster "birth" scene.

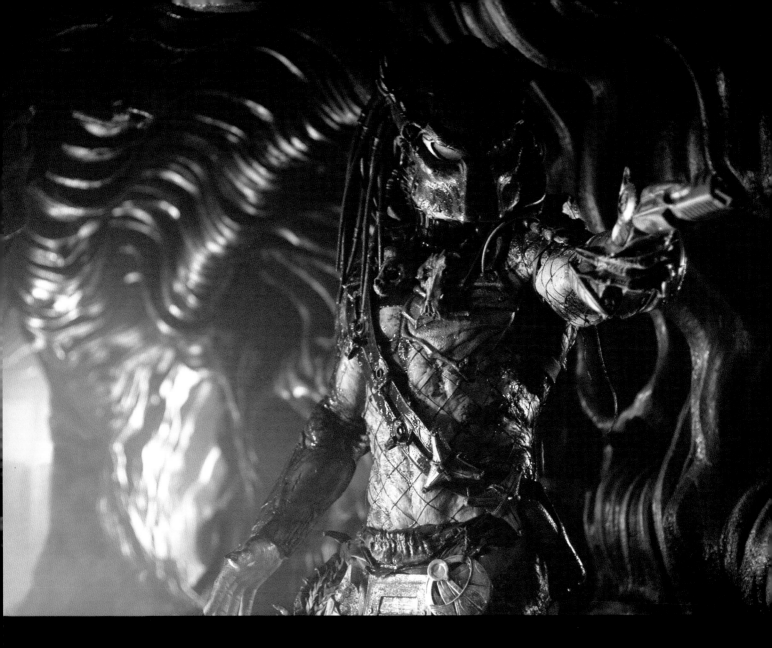

Above: Doc Holliday would be proud as the Predator shows off his gunslinging abilities in the Alien hive.

If the sight of the PredAlien drooling over newborn babies doesn't creep you out, perhaps the method of impregnation will. As written in Shane Salerno's script, the PredAlien regurgitates a half-dozen embryonic Chestbursters down the throats of pregnant women. Not gross enough for you? Did we mention that the PredAlien converts her pregnant belly into a translucent nest of wriggling Alien babies just before they explode from within? All this was accomplished with a specially designed PredAlien head that featured forward-racking mandibles. Shot in reverse, they wrapped around our unfortunate but willing actress, and then undulated obscenely. Another unfortunate but equally willing actress then was installed into a cut-away hospital bed with a translucent silicone belly appliance on top of her and three puppeteers below her.

The Hive

In *Aliens*, Director James Cameron had envisioned the hive as the structure created from the resinous secretions of the Warriors. Serving as protection for the eggs and as a prison for humans with Chestbursters inside them, the hive also works as a metaphor for disease. As if consumed by a cancerous growth, any environment becomes a disgusting and frightening place when infected by the Aliens' handiwork. In story terms it also signifies that our main characters have entered the "belly of the beast." In *AVP2* it is the hospital, which is overtaken, forcing the characters to run through a gauntlet of ravenous creatures in order to get to the helicopter on the roof. As scary as this place is, it's not surprising that the Predator doesn't hesitate to enter. Like a Vietnam War "tunnel rat" when there's a kill to complete, it doesn't matter to the Predator how dark the hole is.

In a practical sense, a set like the hive had to be designed to accommodate the action and a seven-foot-plus man in a Predator suit. Production Designer Andrew Neskoromny and his crew had to make sure that the tunnels were claustrophobic, but not too tight to fit a Predator and a few Aliens. It also had to be sturdy enough to withstand the stunt fighting called for in the script. Carved from Styrofoam and coated with an elastomeric sealant, the set was both functional and organic looking. It was an appropriate setting for Aliens to be blasted with the Predator Shoulder Cannon, shot with rifles, and decapitated with Shurikens. Two of the more elaborate Alien deaths necessitated the stuntmen to be suspended on the walls of the hive wearing specially rigged heads that would remotely slice in two lengthwise. The Shurikens thrown when the Predator kills Jesse were added as digital elements later. One of the great things about the digital tools available on this film is the extra Alien goo that can be added in post-production to increase the "yuck" factor.

Above: The Wolf continues his task of forensic cleansing with a few drops of Dissolving Liquid down the throat of an Alien carcass.

Left: Adam Lisagor uses a dual camera setup to shoot footage showing the Predator's POV. A thermal cam, capable of seeing heat signatures, records the main "Pred-Vision" element while an HD camera picks up high-resolution tracking data and the glowing green Predator blood, which is thermally "invisible."

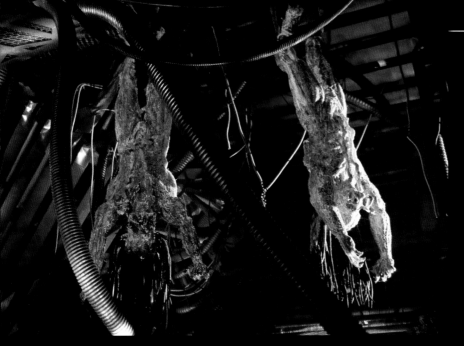

Above: The crew members of the Predator ship we see in the finale of the first *AVP* get a taste of their own lethal medicine when the PredAlien follows his genetically inherited instincts and hangs the skinned corpses of his victims.

Below: One of the skinned Predator dummies, an amalgamation of foam rubber and silicone, waits to be strung up on the crashed ship set.

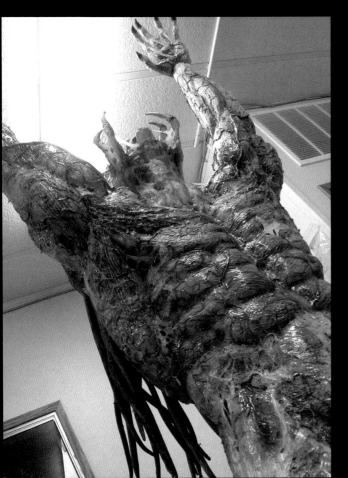

Inside the Crashed Predator Ship

Adjacent to the stage housing, the hive set was the wreck of the Predator escape ship, which in the story has been downed by the PredAlien's ferocious desire to tear things up. The Predator comes upon the still-cloaked wreckage and enters the craft, which has landed upside down. There he sees signs of escaped Facehuggers and two skinned bodies of fellow Predators hanging from the ceiling...er, floor (the set was constructed upside down, making it a precarious working environment). Donning the facemask of another dead compatriot, the Predator gets a fleeting glimpse of an ominous presence, later to be revealed as the PredAlien hybrid. This is also the first time in the movie where the audience gets to see the face of this new Predator.

In this scene we used our cable-articulated Hero Cleaner Case, the equivalent of a spy's weapons valise. Once he's loaded up with Claymore mines, Shurikens, and vials of Dissolving Liquid, he uses his Tracking Syringe to collect Facehugger DNA from a pool of fluid on the ground and inject it into his Wrist Computer. This re-calibrates the Predator-vision in his mask, allowing him to see Facehuggers and the residue they leave behind. Before he embarks on the hunt, he must cover all signs of his presence. The boys in the weapons lab back on the Predator home world have thought of everything because his cleaner case also has a built-in implosion bomb. Insert-shots of the Predator's hand pressing buttons on the Wrist Computer were shot after Ian had been wrapped for the night, so the sharp-eyed viewer might notice that those are Tom's hands wearing the Predator gloves in a couple of quick shots! Add one more character to Tom's resume.

Pickups

On most creature effects movies, there's a list of shots that pile up at the end of the shooting schedule. These are called "pickups" or "inserts." These are the shots that are either too complex and time-consuming for the main period of shooting (e.g., greenscreen shots) or that are isolated enough that they can be postponed and shot as disconnected elements later (e.g., a POV of a Chestburster scuttling by in the sewer). During this time, there are usually multiple camera crews working feverishly to knock off the shots as quickly as possible. At this point, the entire production has condensed down to one shooting stage with elements from many of the scenes set up mere feet from each other. It kind of resembles a theme-park version of the movie: "To your left is the hybrid Chestbursters about to explode from Scar's body; to your right, the Predator staples

Above: Another early victim of the fierce PredAlien.

Right: Yuri Everson paints the Predator's Cleaner Case.

Below: The Wolf reviews video recorded in his fallen comrade's helmet, the Predator version of an aircraft's black box, to gain clues about what caused the crash.

Right: Yuri Everson makes sure a Predator's mask sits properly while shooting pickups.

Below: In Predator culture, Facehuggers have long since replaced goldfish as the pet of choice.

Bottom: Predators escort Facehuggers in stasis tubes across a greenscreen stage (which will be replaced with a CG ship in post). Marc Irvin and Paul Hooson puppeteer the Facehuggers' gross body movements with poles, while Jeny Cassady and Steve Frakes wriggle their tails via monofilament lines.

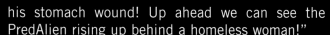

his stomach wound! Up ahead we can see the PredAlien rising up behind a homeless woman!"

Shooting pickups is often when we have the most fun. Up until this point, Yuri Everson and Garth Winkless had been on Main Unit tending to their needs while Tom and Alec were on Second Unit, so it was nice to have all of ADI working under one roof. The frenetic pace and variety of different set-ups was energizing, and as the schedule waned it was a dizzying headlong rush toward the light at the end of the tunnel. The insert phase is always a critical period in the success of the creature work as it provides all the quick cuts that build the action and show the subtleties that make the creatures seem alive. And even though the hectic pace can sometimes mean that we don't get to take the time we want, it's here that we get to work out the intricacies of a Chestburster shedding its skin or depict multiple Predators carrying stasis tubes that hold squirming Facehuggers, for instance. An important component in the inserts on *AVP2* was the huge greenscreen that dominated one section of the stage. It was used to shoot Predators that would later be composited into the interior of the Predator ship before it crashes, and the PredAlien stalking the corridors. Elements of the Predator rising from the lake and the PredAlien menacing Carrie, the pregnant waitress, were also shot in front of the screen. Another corner of the stage housed a section of the rooftop set which was used for a couple of close-ups of actors, and a couple of quick creature cuts, too. This set was dressed with some of the vents and ducting used on the larger exterior rooftop set, and it had a waterproof floor to prevent the rainwater from creeping into the other set pieces. The upside-down crashed Predator ship was still there, as well as a new-and-improved altar upon which a new-and-improved Scar dummy lay—a redux of the last film. There were a couple of half sewer corridors that had been reinstalled as well, and as bad as we had thought that set was, they were a welcomed sight compared to the exterior rooftop location.

After a hectic week of hustling from set-up to set-up, we were almost done. Producer Paul Deason was kind enough to schedule Tom's last suit shot a day early so that he and Alec could catch a plane back to L.A. and attend a 25th anniversary screening of *Aliens* at the Academy of Motion Pictures. While the crew from Cameron's film (including Gale Anne Hurd, Robert and Dennis Skotak, Pat McClung, Shane Mahan, and John Rosengrant) relived old memories in a panel discussion, Yuri Everson, Garth Winkless, Dave Penikas, Kan Ikeuchi, and Marc Irvin finished the last day of pickups on the latest installment in the franchise. Garth stayed on for a couple of weeks supervising a crew of locals in the packing and inventorying of all the parts and pieces, no matter how small. Like Canadian salmon making their way back to their spawning grounds, more than 40 crates of monsters would arrive back at ADI six weeks later. Done.

That is, until the Brothers called saying, "Wouldn't it be cool if we could get just a couple more shots…"

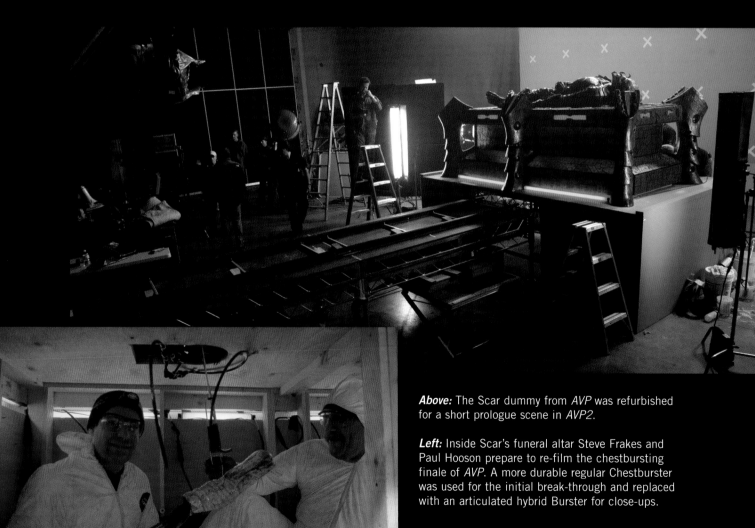

Above: The Scar dummy from *AVP* was refurbished for a short prologue scene in *AVP2*.

Left: Inside Scar's funeral altar Steve Frakes and Paul Hooson prepare to re-film the chestbursting finale of *AVP*. A more durable regular Chestburster was used for the initial break-through and replaced with an articulated hybrid Burster for close-ups.

dark death

All the usual suspects from the Alien world would again be repre-sented, although foregoing an Alien egg this time. Facehuggers would be unleashed upon the human world when live specimens in transit escape from the downed Predator ship.

Wherever possible, we prefer to maintain continuity out of respect for the fans. The Facehuggers were again generated from molds created for *Alien Resurrection*, although the Brothers requested a change to the paint scheme. A key scene in *Aliens* featured a Face-hugger running on extended fingertips across the floor of the Med Lab. The Strause Brothers wanted to take that a step further and see them scurry through the sewers and across the forest floors of our world. To accomplish the goal of keeping the effects real, a sophisticated puppet was built that allowed the fingers to articulate in a rhythmic pattern as if propelling itself by its own power. Batteries kept the fingers moving and tail thrashing from side to side while a puppeteer adjusted the speed via radio control. Although realistically articulated, the fingers could not also take the weight of the Animatronic, so it was either sup-ported from above by monofilament (a simple but reliable old-school approach) or a single cable that ran through a guide inside the puppet from front to back that also allowed us to predetermine its path.

Chestbursters were also revealed in a more gruesome light as they emerge in their own inimitable fashion from father and, for the first time, a child. Two versions of Chestburster puppets accomplished the necessary action. In the first, a rubber skin casting of the creature was quickly inflated while high-pressure blood lines were fired, rupturing a tear-away shirt and providing a bloody reveal. Next, an articulated puppet was attached to the actor's under-clothing harness to writhe and snap its jaws, while blood tubes again provided a wet and hor-rific environment.

Having been such fans of *Aliens*, the Strause Brothers were very partial to that particular iteration of

Previous spread: Crouching in the Gunnison sewer system, an Alien waits for its next victim.

Opposite: In the ADI Finishing Depart-ment, pieces of various materials come together to make up one of sci-fi's most iconic monsters.

Below: Alec Gillis discusses potential ways to subtly change the Alien Warrior's head with Co-Directors Greg and Colin Strause and Executive Producer Paul Deason.

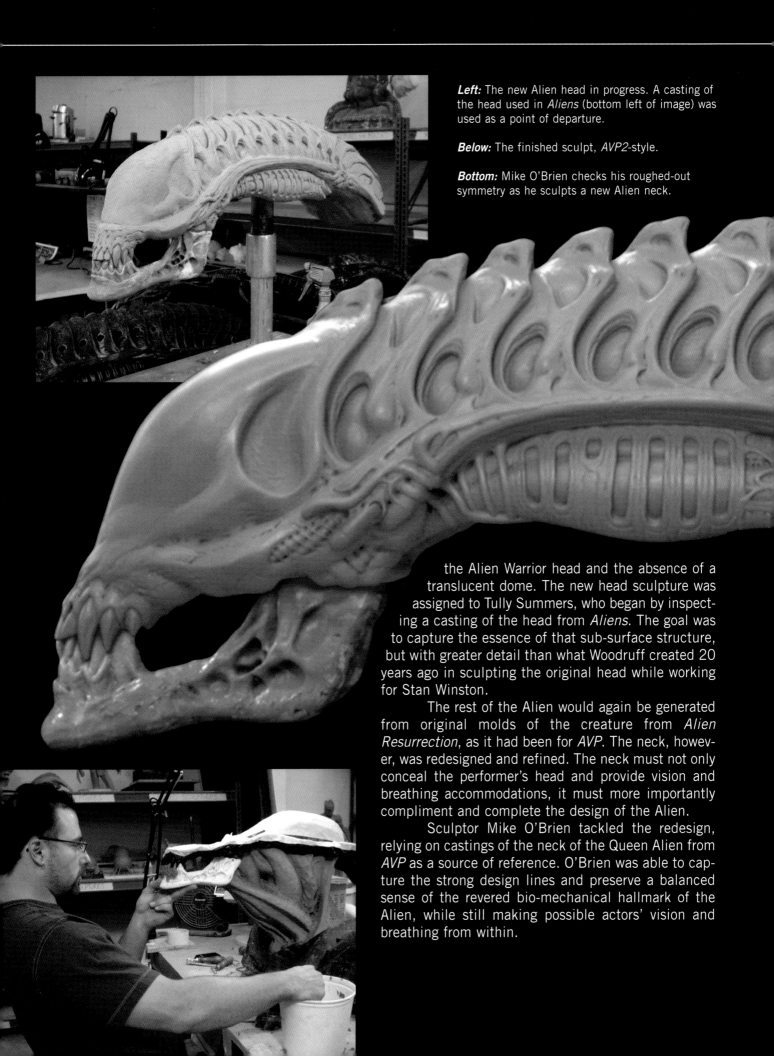

Left: The new Alien head in progress. A casting of the head used in *Aliens* (bottom left of image) was used as a point of departure.

Below: The finished sculpt, *AVP2*-style.

Bottom: Mike O'Brien checks his roughed-out symmetry as he sculpts a new Alien neck.

the Alien Warrior head and the absence of a translucent dome. The new head sculpture was assigned to Tully Summers, who began by inspecting a casting of the head from *Aliens*. The goal was to capture the essence of that sub-surface structure, but with greater detail than what Woodruff created 20 years ago in sculpting the original head while working for Stan Winston.

The rest of the Alien would again be generated from original molds of the creature from *Alien Resurrection*, as it had been for *AVP*. The neck, however, was redesigned and refined. The neck must not only conceal the performer's head and provide vision and breathing accommodations, it must more importantly compliment and complete the design of the Alien.

Sculptor Mike O'Brien tackled the redesign, relying on castings of the neck of the Queen Alien from *AVP* as a source of reference. O'Brien was able to capture the strong design lines and preserve a balanced sense of the revered bio-mechanical hallmark of the Alien, while still making possible actors' vision and breathing from within.

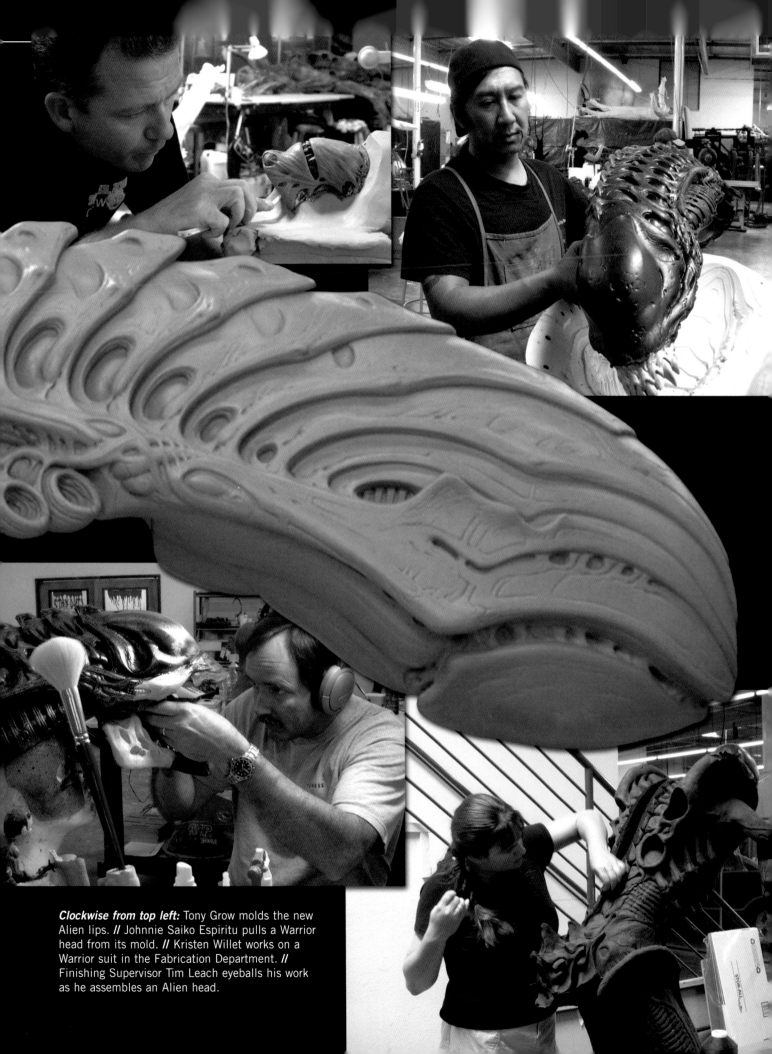

Clockwise from top left: Tony Grow molds the new Alien lips. **//** Johnnie Saiko Espiritu pulls a Warrior head from its mold. **//** Kristen Willet works on a Warrior suit in the Fabrication Department. **//** Finishing Supervisor Tim Leach eyeballs his work as he assembles an Alien head.

Above: Chris Walker attaches tendons to the jaw of an Alien head.

Above right: Rick Galinson makes an adjustment to the inner workings of the Animatronic Facehugger.

Above: Dave Covarrubias works on an Animatronic Warrior head.

Left: Lon Muckey races through the ADI display room with the monofilament-supported, radio-controlled Facehugger as Matt Sheehan shoots some test footage.

Clockwise from top left: Mechanic Rob Derry peers into the underside of the Animatronic Facehugger. // Davis Fandiño uses a vacu-formed template to line up the eyes on a human bust used for the "headburst" scene, in which an Alien's tongue gruesomely punches through a character's head. // The Alien puppet with a pneumatic-ram-powered tongue, which was used for the "headburst" scene. // A cable-operated Chestburster puppet.

Left: After laying down a silver base coat, Mark Maitre starts airbrushing in details on an Alien Warrior.

Below: Koji Ohmura adds color to a forest of Warrior hands.

Bottom: Casey Love paints a trio of Facehuggers.

alien abduction

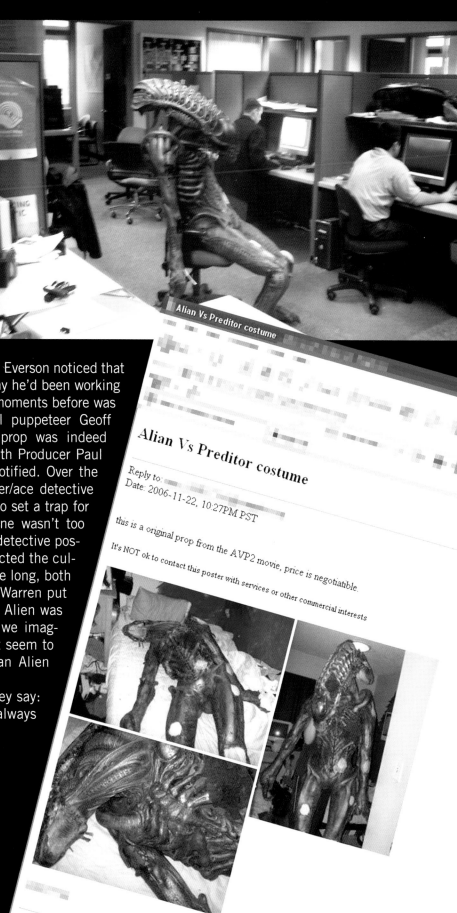

The Internet is a wonderful thing for the movies. It has allowed genre fans to come together with an increased awareness of upcoming films as never before. In the case of *AVP2*, the Internet scuttlebutt of the shooting crew's whereabouts may have helped one young fan achieve his goal of owning a piece of movie magic. But just as the Internet was used to help him try to sell it, it was also used to help the police catch him.

One night while shooting at a high school outside of Vancouver, ADI Supervisor Yuri Everson noticed that the full-body Alien Warrior dummy he'd been working on in the creature effects truck moments before was gone. A calm check with local puppeteer Geoff Redknapp confirmed that the prop was indeed missing. After a quick confab with Producer Paul Deason, the local police were notified. Over the next few days Canadian Producer/ace detective Warren Carr worked with police to set a trap for the thief. As thieves go, this one wasn't too hard to nab. Via the Internet, a detective posing as an interested buyer contacted the culprit and set up a meeting. Before long, both perp and prop were in custody. Warren put it in his passenger seat and the Alien was back in our hands faster than we imagined possible. Other drivers just seem to clear a path when you've got an Alien riding shotgun!

It must be true when they say: the Royal Canadian Mounties always get their man!

Top: One "hot" extraterrestrial awaits pickup in the Vancouver police station.

Right: The web page offering the dummy for sale.

Alian Vs Preditor costume

Alian Vs Preditor costume

Reply to:
Date: 2006-11-22, 10:27PM PST

this is a original prop from the AVP2 movie, price is negotiable.

It's NOT ok to contact this poster with services or other commercial interests

I've had the good fortune to play many monster roles over the last 20 years and get out to the conventions to meet the people most interested in the work I do. It's a treat to see the people on the other side of the table that are just as I used to be, like so many years ago when I took a bus to New York City for the first *Famous Monsters* convention back in 1974. While the questions are often the same, the enthusiasm and interest in what it's like to play the Alien always makes it interesting. And while I'm constantly reminding myself that I have one of the best jobs a person could want, it's not always easy to remember how lucky I am—especially on those long, cold night shoots outdoors.

Sitting there in our little temporary office built on an empty soundstage at two in the morning, waiting for the call to suit up, I don't feel anything like lucky. The suit is still damp and cold from the night before, when I spent hours being soaked by heavy rains. The constant action in the wet environment of the sewer set and outdoors in the rain has taken its toll on the suits, and clean, dry replacements are hardly a common occurrence. We normally use a lot of talcum powder to be able to slip into the custom body suits, but under these circumstances it quickly cakes up and leave a chalky residue everywhere (yes, *everywhere*). As the night wears on, it doesn't help to hope that they won't get to my scene. If we don't get to it tonight, it will only mean prolonging the shoot, or worse, losing valuable screen time for the Alien. I have to remind myself that this is something I've wanted to do since I was a kid— and something I take pride in: the performance skills I've developed and the professional reputation I've earned.

Our suit driers are turned on high, blasting hot air into the suit through the open back and sleeves like over-sized hair driers. But they only serve to overload the electric circuits in the room, tripping the breakers and shutting everything down: driers, computers, and lights. A flashlight leads the way to the opposite corner of stage to put the lights back on.

There is no heat in this partitioned room with its ceiling open to the entire stage space. It's cold enough that I start to shiver, even with multiple layers of sweatshirts and a coat. As I'm thinking that this would be the worst time to have to climb into the suit, already chilled, I hear the door open and the walkie-talkie of the first AD before she even knocks on the door. "Call the Alien to the set."

It's going to be many months before I'm warm and dry again, sitting behind a table and explaining what it's like to play the Alien. And agreeing, really agreeing, that yeah, it is a lucky thing that I get to wear that rubber suit.

—*Tom Woodruff, Jr.*

Left: Tom Woodruff, Jr. rehearses a shot with actress Gina Holden in the diner kitchen.

like father, like son(s)

Photo courtesy of the Frakes Historical Society

M y three sons have been around the workshop since they were children. But before you conjure up images of Fred MacMurray's wingtips tapping to a spiffy harmonica riff, ours was not a sitcom slice of life. My kids were the ones in the school Halloween parade wearing masks I'd made of retro classics like *The Creature from the Black Lagoon* or *The Mole People* while their friends were Power Rangers or ninjas. Their classic "dare" was to turn off the lights in the ADI display room and see who could bravely walk from one end to the other without breaking into a run. But they did host some of the coolest second-grade field trips, complete with a photo of each holding an Oscar! It was a real Harry Chapin moment to now see two of them grown and working in the shop— one off to college and the other close to finishing high school. Maybe an *AVP3* will see the last one, Connor, get his hands dirty yet...

—*TW, Jr.*

Top: If American cinema had grown up in rural Pennsylvania instead of Hollywood, the early days of the creature effects trade may have looked something like this.

Left: David (left) and Taylor carry on the Woodruff monster-making tradition.

the wolf

There's a challenge to creating a Predator that has its own individual character, and as each film featuring these interstellar hunters comes along, the challenge becomes greater. In *Predator* we saw the creature for the first time. He was a cunning hunter, a sadistic killer, a mimic, and ultimately a spoilsport with a wrist nuke. In our minds he was the youngest of all the Predators we've since seen; a precocious brat dropped on a planet of soft, easily frightened beings that really were no match for him—with the obvious exception of Arnold. In the second film we saw Predator Elders and the now famous Alien skull on display inside their spaceship. *AVP*'s Predators were a group of "teens" on the cusp of adulthood, being tested for the first time against the universe's deadliest killing machine: the Alien.

With the latest installment in the series we have a Predator who is like no other. He's a veteran of many missions, a loner whose history is written in his battle-worn armor and scarred flesh. He's an archetypal character we've seen in different guises in various genres. He's part Harvey Keitel in *Pulp Fiction*, part Willem Dafoe in *Platoon*. He's a bit of the Eastwood-like Mysterious Stranger of the Spaghetti Western, or Kurosawa's Lone Samurai striding into town to take care of business. He's not in the flower of his youth either. Our vision of the Wolf was that if he were human he'd be a guy in his forties, still in great physical condition, but perhaps at this point in his life he'd be relying a little more on brains than brawn. When you're in the business of hunting Aliens, the dumb don't live long.

Previous spread: Just doing his job. The Wolf hunts Aliens in the sewer system of a small Colorado town.

Opposite: Farzad Varahramyan captures the blue-collar toughness and overall attitude of the new Predator character.

Right: Greg Figiel's maquette, featuring facial scarring and a missing mandible, suggest that this Predator has seen better days.

Right: During pre-production design meetings with ADI co-owners Alec Gillis and Tom Woodruff, Jr. and the Strause Brothers, concept art, maquettes, and reference material from previous *Alien* and *Predator* films were critiqued and discussed to develop the look of the characters and props for *AVP2*. (Concept art by Farzad Varahramyan, maquette by Steve Wang.)

Below: Predator concept art by Michael Broom.

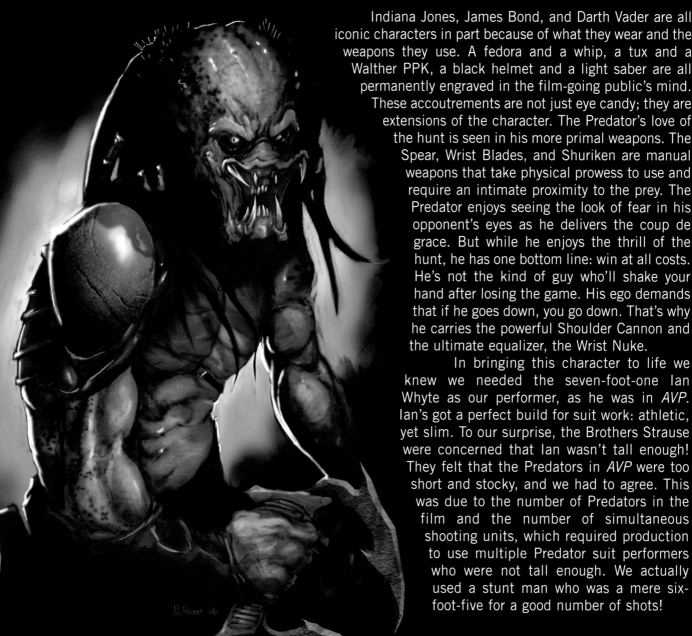

Indiana Jones, James Bond, and Darth Vader are all iconic characters in part because of what they wear and the weapons they use. A fedora and a whip, a tux and a Walther PPK, a black helmet and a light saber are all permanently engraved in the film-going public's mind. These accoutrements are not just eye candy; they are extensions of the character. The Predator's love of the hunt is seen in his more primal weapons. The Spear, Wrist Blades, and Shuriken are manual weapons that take physical prowess to use and require an intimate proximity to the prey. The Predator enjoys seeing the look of fear in his opponent's eyes as he delivers the coup de grace. But while he enjoys the thrill of the hunt, he has one bottom line: win at all costs. He's not the kind of guy who'll shake your hand after losing the game. His ego demands that if he goes down, you go down. That's why he carries the powerful Shoulder Cannon and the ultimate equalizer, the Wrist Nuke.

In bringing this character to life we knew we needed the seven-foot-one Ian Whyte as our performer, as he was in *AVP*. Ian's got a perfect build for suit work: athletic, yet slim. To our surprise, the Brothers Strause were concerned that Ian wasn't tall enough! They felt that the Predators in *AVP* were too short and stocky, and we had to agree. This was due to the number of Predators in the film and the number of simultaneous shooting units, which required production to use multiple Predator suit performers who were not tall enough. We actually used a stunt man who was a mere six-foot-five for a good number of shots!

(Continued on page 69)

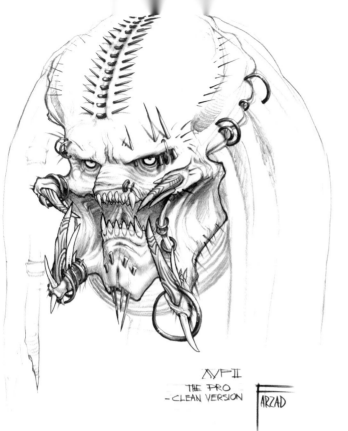

AVPII
THE PRO
- CLEAN VERSION
Farzad

AVPII
THE PRO
- CLEAN VERSION
Farzad

This page: Farzad Varahramyan explored a variety of treatments for the Wolf's face, including tribal piercings, tattoos, and disfigurement from previous battles.

Following spread:

Left: Predator design maquette by Jordu Schell.

Right: Artwork by Farzad Varahramyan.

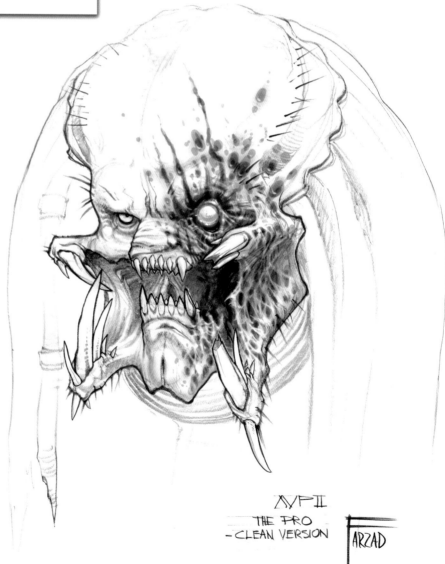

AVPII
THE PRO
- CLEAN VERSION
Farzad

Right: In a carryover from the design phase on the first *AVP*, Farzad Varahramyan's concept of Battle Claws was again proposed as a possible addition to the Predator's arsenal.

Below left: Predator concept art by Michael Broom. One of the design mandates on this film was for a less armor-clad Predator.

Below right: Armor concept art by Farzad Varahramyan.

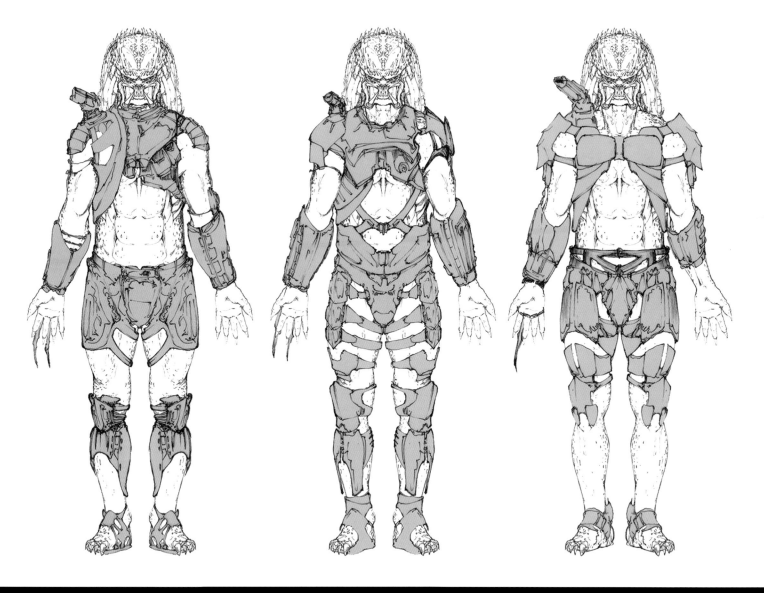

(Continued from page 64)

Once the Brothers understood this, they realized that the proportion problem in the previous film would be solved by more screen time with Ian Whyte, not less. In *AVP2* there was to be virtually only one Predator. Knowing this, we were able to take full advantage of Ian's proportions and create a much sleeker body suit. We also wanted to re-proportion the face, giving the brow a more cunning, sweptback angle, like a predatory cat. To accomplish this we knew we needed mechanical eyes instead of Ian's eyes, and that he would be performing blind during the entire end fight sequence—risky, but well worth the design improvements.

Top: Various armor concepts by Chris Howe.

Right: In addition to the hammered metal texture of previous *Predator* films, intricate filigree scrollwork was incorporated into the Wolf's armor.

No doubt there will be those who watch this film and see no difference between this and any previous incarnation of the Predator, and in a way, that's a good thing. It means that our design modifications are subtle and respectful of the original, not arrogantly or arbitrarily different for the sake of change. We hope that the astute viewer will see that little bit of attitude or extra life that makes this Predator live as a character worthy of the name *the Wolf*.

Top: Davis Fandiño focuses his attention on a Predator foot.

Above: The finished head sculpt.

Right: In his first stint at ADI, longtime industry veteran Joey Orosco nears completion on the face of the new Predator character.

Above left: Joey Orosco roughs out one of the Predator's massive mitts.

Above right: Hiroshi Katagiri and Joey Orosco sculpt the new Predator over a life cast of performer Ian Whyte.

Left: The finished hand sculpture, complete with a Predator-version of brass knuckles.

makers play a key role in the creation of ADI's creatures.
produce the elaborate molds that allow the precise replication
e fragile clay sculptures in a variety of materials.

ve: Gary Pawlowski comes face to face with the Predator as
nolds its head.

t: Brian Van Dorn brushes a releasing agent onto a Predator hand.

w: Gary Pawlowski and Steve Munson dry a coat of shellac
re molding the Pred body in fiberglass.

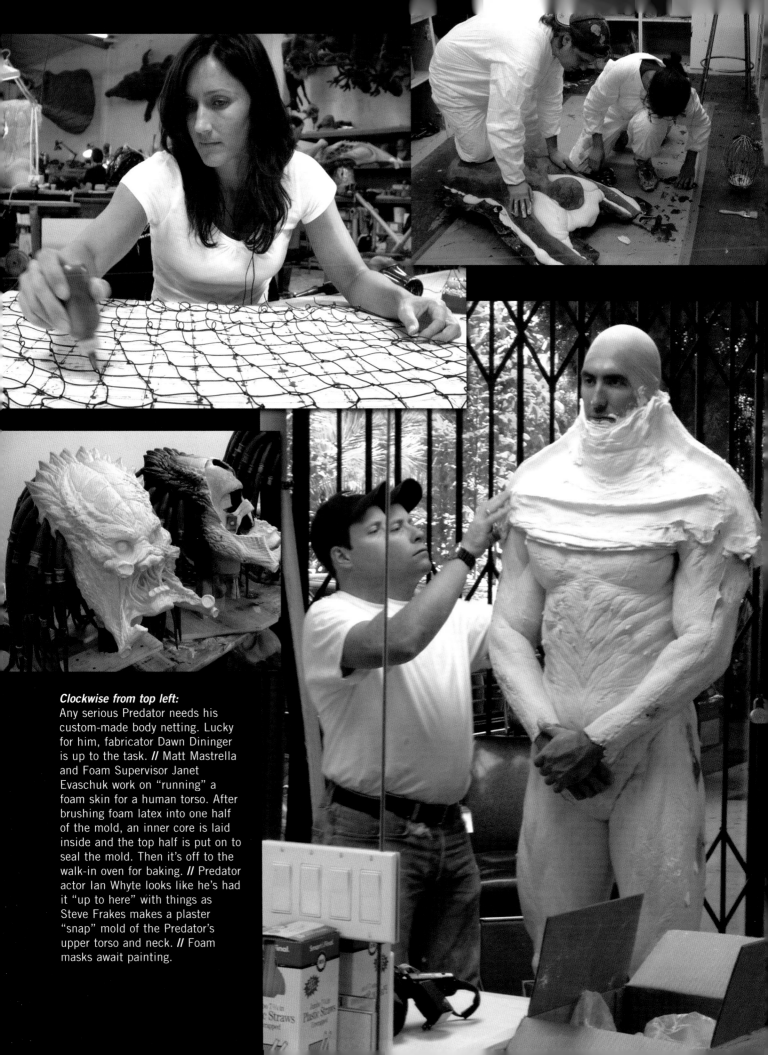

Clockwise from top left:
Any serious Predator needs his custom-made body netting. Lucky for him, fabricator Dawn Dininger is up to the task. **//** Matt Mastrella and Foam Supervisor Janet Evaschuk work on "running" a foam skin for a human torso. After brushing foam latex into one half of the mold, an inner core is laid inside and the top half is put on to seal the mold. Then it's off to the walk-in oven for baking. **//** Predator actor Ian Whyte looks like he's had it "up to here" with things as Steve Frakes makes a plaster "snap" mold of the Predator's upper torso and neck. **//** Foam masks await painting.

Clockwise from top: No need to give Suma Abuzaineh a big hand for helping bring the creatures of *AVP2* to life—she already has one. // Penny Jane Mackie tenderizes leather to give the Wolf's costume a distressed and worn look. // Ian Whyte and Garth Winkless in an early suit test fitting.

England in the seventies and eighties was not ready for anyone who stood out from the crowd as much as I did. As a child, I longed for something to release me from the pressure of constant bullying and ridicule that I had to endure. The game of basketball was that release. I found a use for my height, a passion, and a longed-for freedom of expression that no longer attracted ridicule from playground bullies.

After nine years in the NCAA, I finally called it quits on a professional career, which had taken me all over Europe, New Zealand, and the Azores. Generally speaking, though, I found the business of sport to be a one-way street. What started off as an escape turned into a passion, and finally ended up driving me to the brink of despair. Then something completely unforeseen happened. I received a call offering me the part of the Predator in *AVP*. Even after a grueling casting process, I still didn't know that I had just taken my first step towards a new career.

In my opinion there isn't anything special about being over seven-feet tall. It's a small hindrance sometimes when traveling by plane, great for helping little old ladies in the supermarket, but generally nothing to sing and dance about. However, being presented with an opportunity to portray one of the most iconic monsters ever devised for the screen is something to sing and dance about.

Much has been said and written about the difficulty of playing costume roles in general and the Predator in particular. Performing a character that has no face to speak of and does not emote through language is a luxury for an actor like me who does not have the benefit of classical training. The costume, although well designed, is hot, dirty, smelly, and an inconvenience in every way you can imagine. It's an action role, which means that for most of the time I'm very tired and sometimes uncomfortably close to heat exhaustion and lack of oxygen. That, dear hearts, is the business of costume performance.

Despite the difficulties of the role, I learned very early on the importance of being emotionally involved with the character. Although the role is characterized by its physicality rather than its emotion, it is so much more than just a rubber costume. The character has soul and depth, and it is the task of the actor to plumb those depths and breath life into it as though it were a living organism.

Close to the end of filming on *AVP2*, I was asked if I ever reached the point of exhaustion when I didn't care about the role any more. The simple answer is no. The principles of a costume role are the same as those of a dramatic one. The day that you stop caring about your performance is the day that you don't deserve to do the job anymore.

—Ian Whyte

Left: Ian Whyte pauses for a brief moment of reflection before donning that iconic mask for the next shot.

Above: The Killen Brothers, Johnathon and Matt, mirror each other as they glue armor to Predator hands.

Above: The internal eye mechanism for the Animatronic Predator head.

Right: Lon Muckey and Chris Wolters perform a mechanical lobotomy on the Animatronic Pred head.

Right: Paint Supervisor Mike Larrabee devised a paint scheme on a third-scale maquette (leftover from *AVP*) before tackling the full-sized head.

Below: Koji Ohmura assures that the Predator's armory is well stocked. Multiple Predator suits, armor, and weapons were created to endure the harsh conditions of the shoot.

Left: A Predator suit begins to take shape under the guidance of painter Brian Clawson.

WEAPONS

shoulder cannon

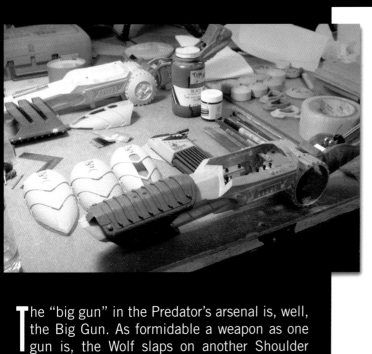

The "big gun" in the Predator's arsenal is, well, the Big Gun. As formidable a weapon as one gun is, the Wolf slaps on another Shoulder Cannon when he realizes he's up against the PredAlien, an opponent of unknown abilities. This time around we've streamlined the weapon, added a recharge lighting display, a recoil feature, and a clip-on handle for hand-held use. Double the body count—double the fun!

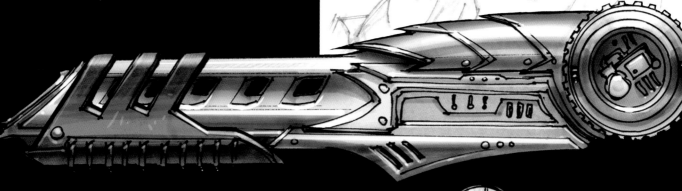

Clockwise from upper left: Various gun model pieces cover Tim Arp's desk. // Early concept art by Farzad Varahramyan explores an unused idea of placing actual gun holsters on the Predator's back. // Shoulder Cannon design by Varahramyan. // A meeting of the minds as Bob Mano and Tim Arp discuss gun mechanics.

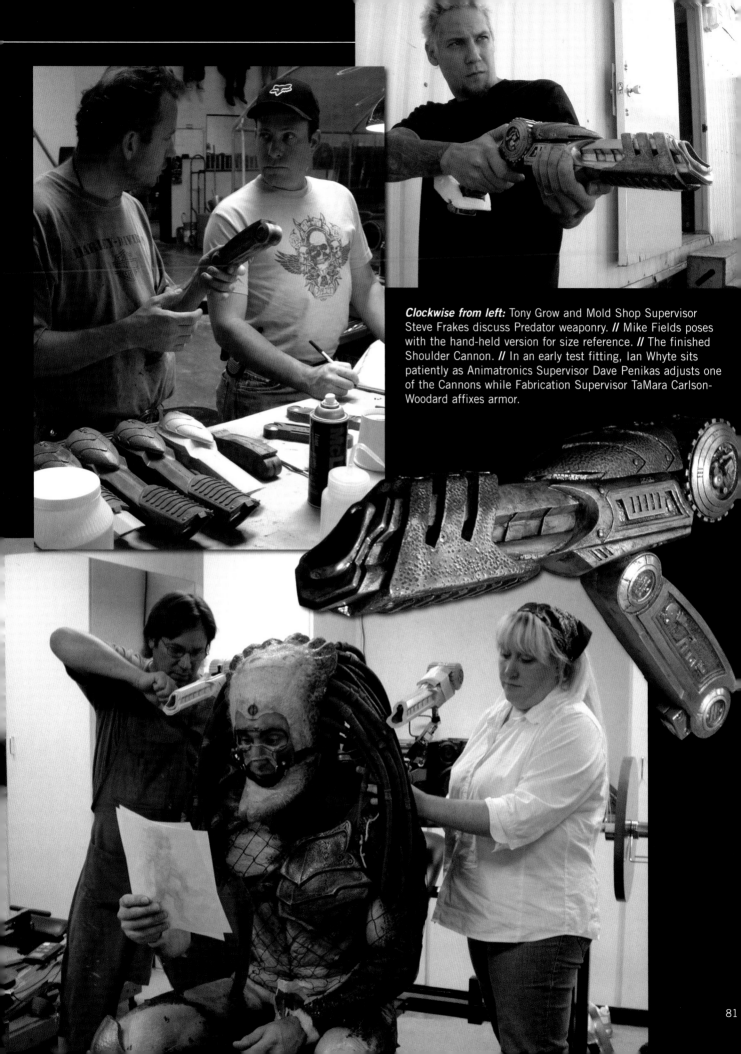

Clockwise from left: Tony Grow and Mold Shop Supervisor Steve Frakes discuss Predator weaponry. // Mike Fields poses with the hand-held version for size reference. // The finished Shoulder Cannon. // In an early test fitting, Ian Whyte sits patiently as Animatronics Supervisor Dave Penikas adjusts one of the Cannons while Fabrication Supervisor TaMara Carlson-Woodard affixes armor.

whip

One of Farzad's early concept sketches showed a "bull-whip" hanging off the Predator's hip. As a simple, almost primitive weapon, the whip shows the skill and grace of the universe's ultimate hunter. The razor-sharp teeth are designed to slice an Alien in two, and more than one of them loses its head to the Wolf's (and Ian Whyte's) skills.

Above: Concept art of the whip in action by Michael Broom.

Left: Sculptor Mark Maitre methodically works his way through the whip's many toothed links.

Below: The design exploration process included this version by Farzad Varahramyan that could recoil into the handle. It also featured an Alien tail tip at the end.

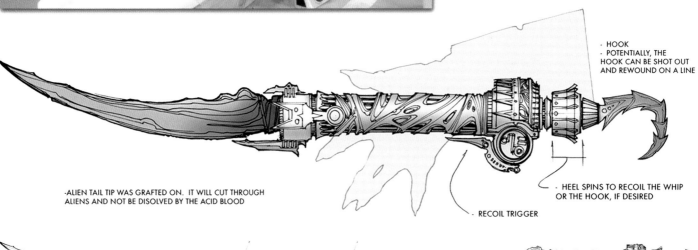

- HOOK
- POTENTIALLY, THE HOOK CAN BE SHOT OUT AND REWOUND ON A LINE

-ALIEN TAIL TIP WAS GRAFTED ON. IT WILL CUT THROUGH ALIENS AND NOT BE DISOLVED BY THE ACID BLOOD

- HEEL SPINS TO RECOIL THE WHIP OR THE HOOK, IF DESIRED

- RECOIL TRIGGER

- WHIP CAN EXTEND TO A VARIETY OF LENGTHS DETERMINED BY THE TASK AT HAND

Top (and insets): Ten feet of nastiness—the finished whip.

Above: Chris Carey cleans up a casting of the whip handle.

Left: Like an otherworldly snake charmer, Matt Killen wrangles a foam rubber whip into shape.

power punch

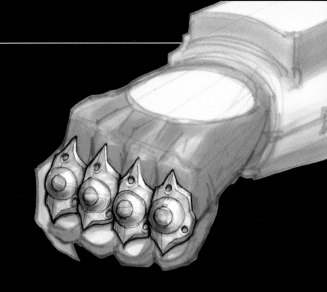

The Wolf's first encounter with the PredAlien leaves him dazed, confused, and ten feet under the ground in Gunnison's sewer system. The quickest way out is to punch right through solid concrete! As strong as he is, even a Predator occasionally needs help in the form of a metal bridge between his computer gauntlet and his "brass knuckles."

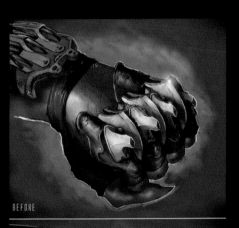

BEFORE

AFTER

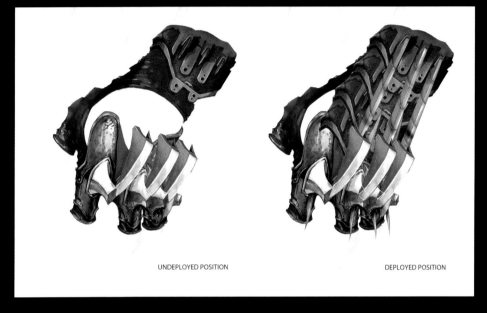

UNDEPLOYED POSITION

DEPLOYED POSITION

Top three images: Various designs for the Power Punch glove by Michael Broom.

Right: At one point in the design phase, the Power Punch feature was going to involve the Predator's entire left arm. His existing armor would transform and expand, including flanges that flared out to shield him from splattering Alien acid blood. Art by Farzad Varahramyan.

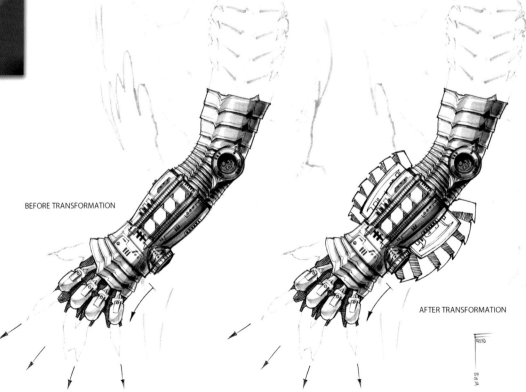

BEFORE TRANSFORMATION

AFTER TRANSFORMATION

Left: A gloved Brian Clawson paints a gloved Predator.

Below: The Power Punch glove was sculpted in clay on a resin cast of the Predator's hand to ensure maximum precision.

Below: *Ka-Boom!* The Predator creates his own exit from the sewer tunnel below.

Below right: Talk about potholes. The Wolf emerges onto the streets of Gunnison.

Cleaner Case

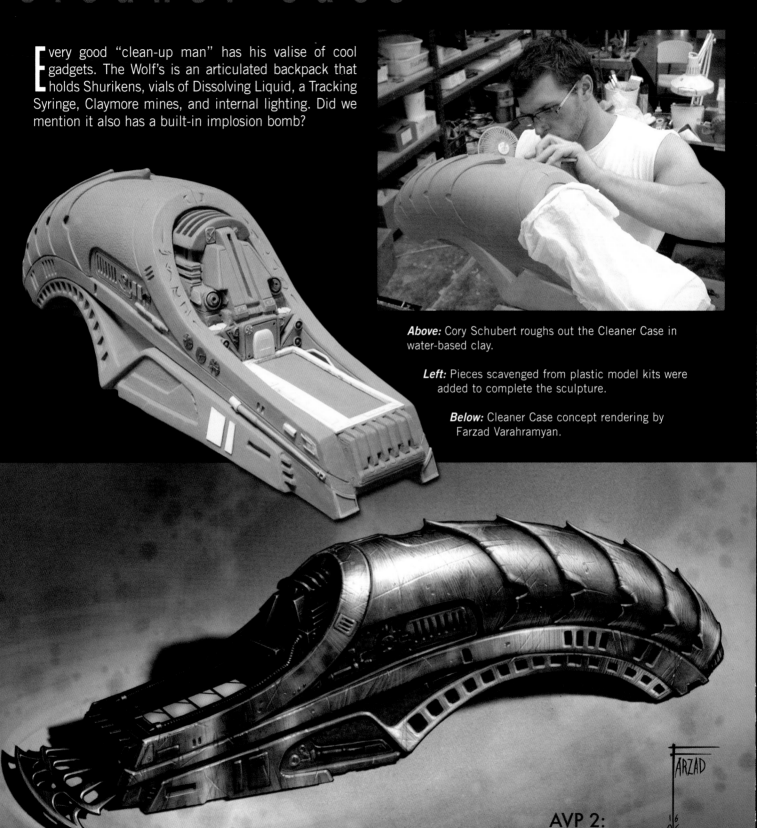

Every good "clean-up man" has his valise of cool gadgets. The Wolf's is an articulated backpack that holds Shurikens, vials of Dissolving Liquid, a Tracking Syringe, Claymore mines, and internal lighting. Did we mention it also has a built-in implosion bomb?

Above: Cory Schubert roughs out the Cleaner Case in water-based clay.

Left: Pieces scavenged from plastic model kits were added to complete the sculpture.

Below: Cleaner Case concept rendering by Farzad Varahramyan.

AVP 2:
CLEANER CASE

Clockwise from above: Using foam dummy props, Assistant Shop Supervisor Garth Winkless works out the best way to fit the Predator's many tools and weapons into the case. **//** Gary Pawlowski adds shims to the Cleaner Case mold. **//** Horacio Fernandez inspects a fiberglass casting before handing it off to the Finishing Department. **//** The finished prop waits to be delivered to the set.

The Wolf's mission is to erase all signs of Aliens in our world by using specialized tools. With the Tracking Syringe, he injects Facehugger DNA into his Wrist Computer in order to calibrate his Predator-Vision, enabling him to see them. Vials of Dissolving Liquid ensure that all that's left of a dead Alien is a pile of goop. If things get crazy, motion-sensing Claymore mines can dissolve multiple Aliens at once!

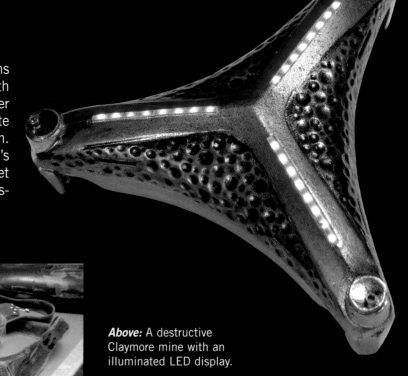

Above: A destructive Claymore mine with an illuminated LED display.

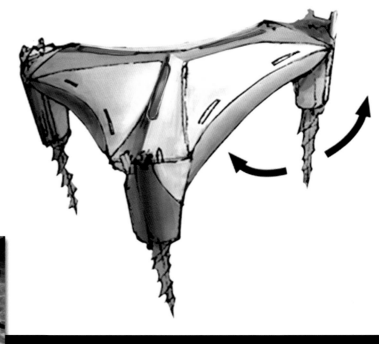

Above left: Claymores get attached to the Wolf's bandolier in the Fabrication Department.

Above right: Chris Howe's concept art of a Claymore depicts extendable screws able to burrow into a target's surface.

Left: Matt Killen attaches "feet" to resin Claymore castings.

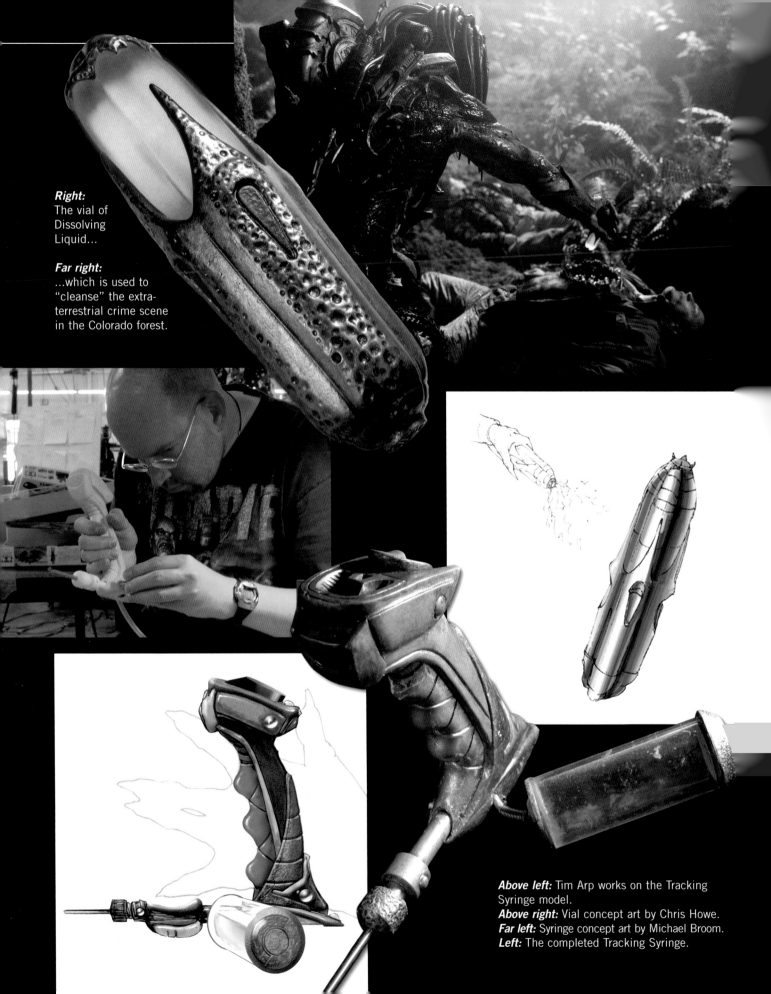

Right:
The vial of Dissolving Liquid...

Far right:
...which is used to "cleanse" the extra-terrestrial crime scene in the Colorado forest.

Above left: Tim Arp works on the Tracking Syringe model.
Above right: Vial concept art by Chris Howe.
Far left: Syringe concept art by Michael Broom.
Left: The completed Tracking Syringe.

helmet

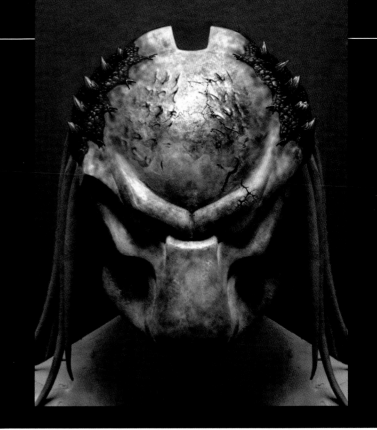

Deceivingly simple in design, the helmet is the iconic "face" of the Predator for most of the movie. This time around its narrower eyes, jutting jaw, and sweptback forehead denote a character that is more cunning and ruthless than any we've seen before. Carved runes and imbedded teeth of past prey show a history of previous missions accomplished by this lone hunter. As battle ravaged as this mask is, the face beneath it shows more proof of the risks of hunting Aliens.

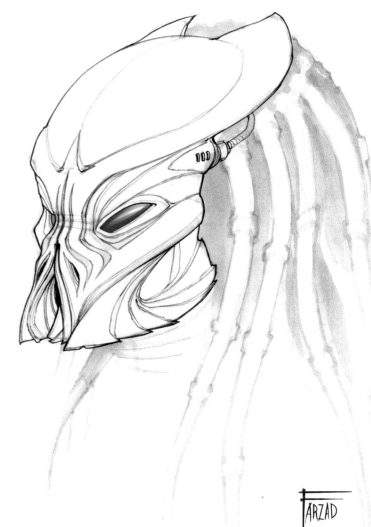

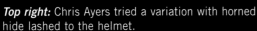

Top right: Chris Ayers tried a variation with horned hide lashed to the helmet.

Above: One of Michael Broom's designs used a trophy skull for part of the helmet.

Right: Helmet concept art by Farzad Varahramyan.

Opposite page: Carlos Huante, Justin Murray, Farzad Varahramyan, and Chris Howe explore a variety of shapes and textures in helmet designs.

Clockwise from top left: A variety of Predator helmet maquettes sculpted by Steve Wang, Mark Maitre, Greg Figiel, and Cory Schubert. Wang's design replaced the traditional three-point laser-sighting device, as seen in previous Predator films, with a script-like design in the middle of the brow. Directors Colin and Greg Strause chose to base the final piece predominantly on Schubert's maquette.

Opposite: Hiroshi Katagiri attends to the nearly completed helmet sculpture.

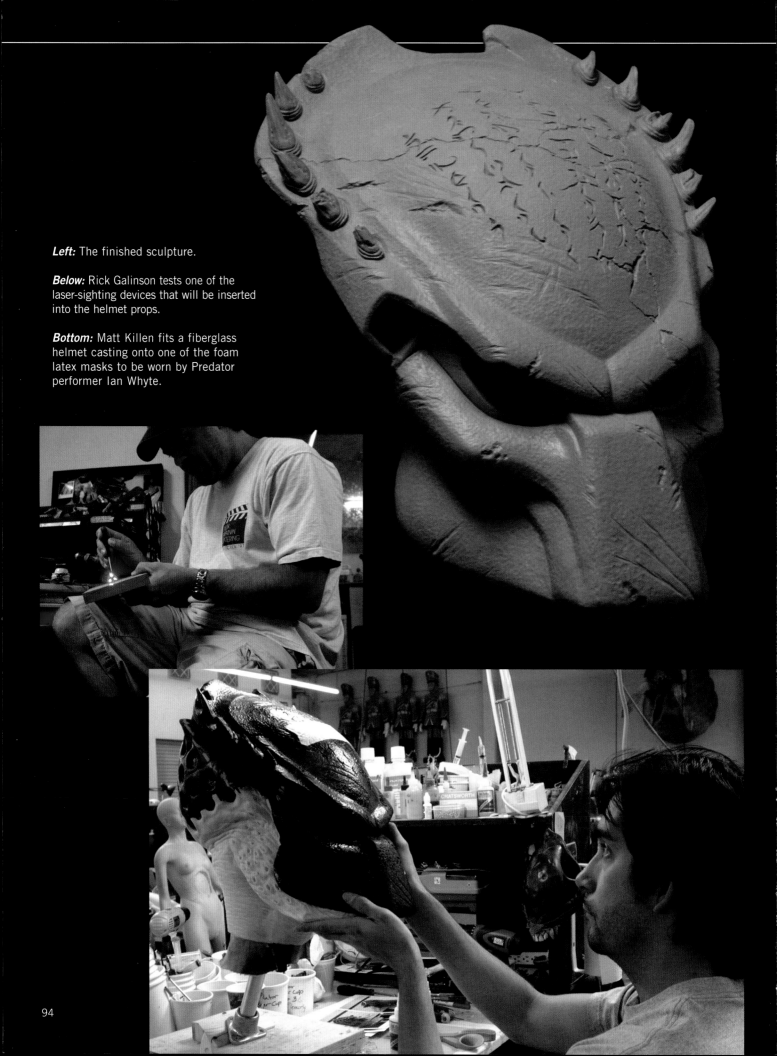

Left: The finished sculpture.

Below: Rick Galinson tests one of the laser-sighting devices that will be inserted into the helmet props.

Bottom: Matt Killen fits a fiberglass helmet casting onto one of the foam latex masks to be worn by Predator performer Ian Whyte.

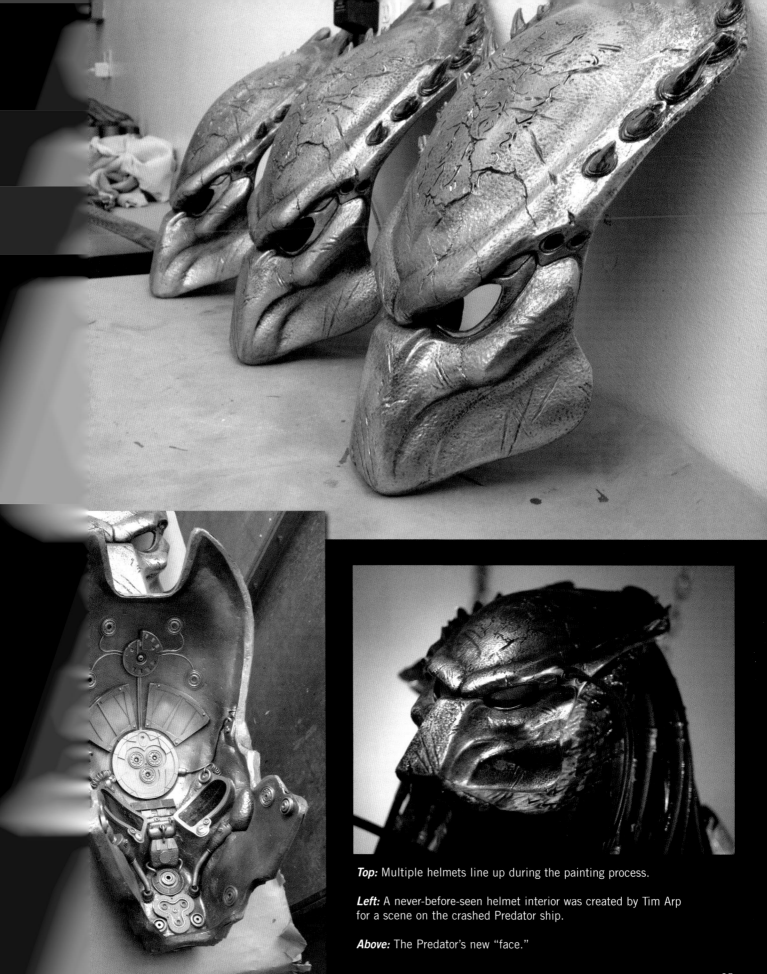

Top: Multiple helmets line up during the painting process.

Left: A never-before-seen helmet interior was created by Tim Arp for a scene on the crashed Predator ship.

Above: The Predator's new "face."

med kit

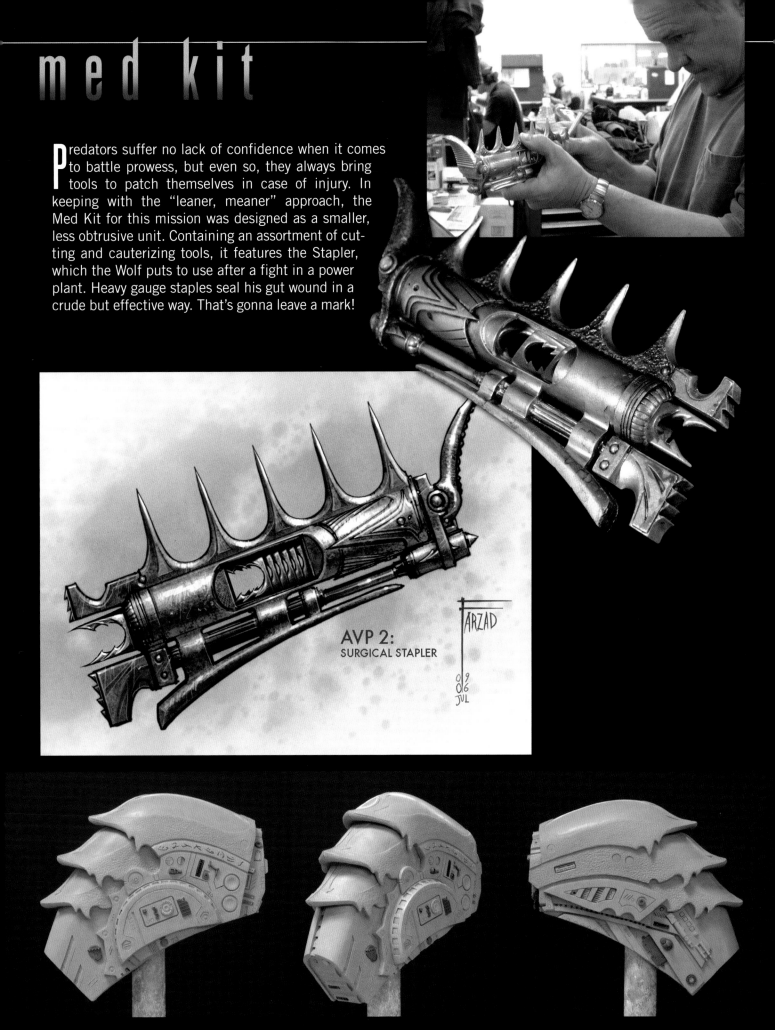

Predators suffer no lack of confidence when it comes to battle prowess, but even so, they always bring tools to patch themselves in case of injury. In keeping with the "leaner, meaner" approach, the Med Kit for this mission was designed as a smaller, less obtrusive unit. Containing an assortment of cutting and cauterizing tools, it features the Stapler, which the Wolf puts to use after a fight in a power plant. Heavy gauge staples seal his gut wound in a crude but effective way. That's gonna leave a mark!

AVP 2:
SURGICAL STAPLER

FARZAD
01 9
06
JUL

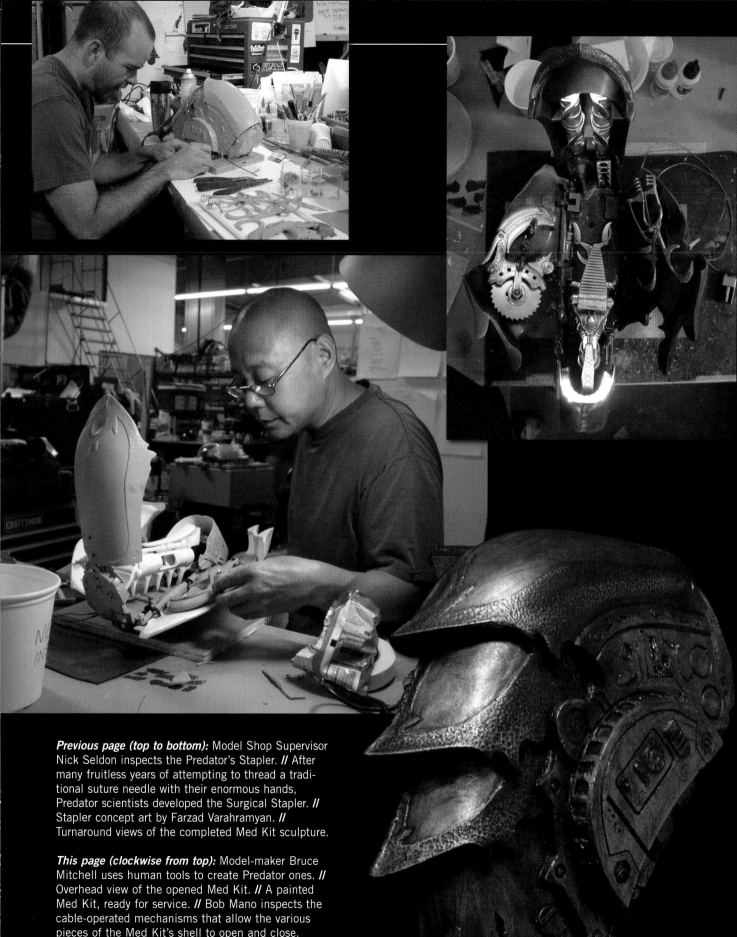

Previous page (top to bottom): Model Shop Supervisor Nick Seldon inspects the Predator's Stapler. // After many fruitless years of attempting to thread a traditional suture needle with their enormous hands, Predator scientists developed the Surgical Stapler. // Stapler concept art by Farzad Varahramyan. // Turnaround views of the completed Med Kit sculpture.

This page (clockwise from top): Model-maker Bruce Mitchell uses human tools to create Predator ones. // Overhead view of the opened Med Kit. // A painted Med Kit, ready for service. // Bob Mano inspects the cable-operated mechanisms that allow the various pieces of the Med Kit's shell to open and close.

tried and true

Although the Wolf has some new weapons and gadgets, he still relies on the tried-and-true tools of his trade that have become the hallmark of the Predator arsenal. The Telescoping Spear, the Shuriken, and the Wrist Blades are all put to good use once again, while the Wrist Computer provides increased tracking abilities, helping this Predator to relentlessly pursue his prey. The Wrist Computer's explosive feature ensures that the nuclear option is always on the table. Other weapons such as exploding Bolas and Battle Claws didn't make it on this mission, but may be included in the Predator's weapons cache in the future!

Above: Mike O'Brien listens to feedback as Shop Supervisor Yuri Everson, Tom Woodruff, Jr., and Alec Gillis do a shop walkthrough to check on the status of things.

Left: The Wolf bares his lethal Wrist Blades.

Below: In between the molding and painting stages, Sherry Angelo cleans and details a Wrist Blade.

Above: The Wrist Computer housing and LED display.
Below: All systems go! The finished prop on set.

Above: Nick Seldon tries the Wrist Computer on for size...

Below: ...but it seems to fit the real thing a little better.

Above: Gary Pawlowski molds a retracted Spear.
Right: Johnathon Killen patches a Spear cast in resin.

Left: The Predator's Spear aids him in his rooftop encounter with the PredAlien.

Below: A trio of freshly painted Spears dries in the paint room spray booth.

Opposite: The Wolf stands ready for battle... or to pick up a new pair of cross-trainers.

a new terror

About a year before we began production on *AVP2* we got a call from Producer John Davis with a heads up that the project might be coming our way. As is often the case in Hollywood, you see the plume of smoke long before the train arrives. That said, sometimes enthusiasm takes over and you just have to go where it takes you, so we thought we'd generate a couple of PredAlien designs. Alec had an idea for a Queen-like version and he sculpted a head using castings of teeth from our miniature Queen from *AVP*. For dreadlocks, he cast multiple tails from the molds of the miniature Alien from Fincher's *Alien3*, and heat-formed them into shape. Artist Steve Koch then photographed the sculpture and digitally added mandibles from the Predator in ADI's showroom and gave the creature the appropriate paint scheme.

Previous spread: Slick and slimy—the PredAlien in all its gooey glory.

Opposite: An early PredAlien design by Farzad Varahramyan.

Below: PredAlien design maquette by Jordu Schell.

Top: Steve Koch's Photoshop artwork (based on Jordu Schell's maquette) shows the immense proposed scale of the PredAlien.

Above: PredAlien design by Michael Broom.

Meanwhile, Tom worked with frequent ADI collaborator Jordu Schell on a full body maquette of another version of the PredAlien. This one leaned a bit more towards the Predator aesthetic, particularly in the anatomy of the body. Again working with Steve Koch, the maquette was photographed and composited into a shot towering over a human.

The real design work didn't start until all the elements were in place, namely a script and the directors. At that point we were able to sit down with Colin and Greg Strause and do what we always do when a job starts: We listen. It's very important in supporting a director's vision to understand where he or she is coming from: what he or she liked about the previous *Alien* and *Predator* films, and perhaps more importantly, what he or she disliked. One of the great things about these characters is that they generate strong opinions. Since we are not the original designers, we consider ourselves caretakers of these classic creatures, but we are also responsible to the story and the director's vision for this constantly evolving franchise.

Fox executive Alex Young, Producer John Davis, and the Strauses were all in agreement that since this new creature was an Alien that had gestated inside a Predator, it may have picked up traits from its host but was fundamentally still an Alien. Our logic on *Alien³* was similar for the "dog" Alien, but this time we all felt that the potent DNA of the host Predator might cause more intermixing of traits. This allowed us to play more with the superficial features like dreadlocks, mandibles, and coloration. Due to the tight production schedule, the design meetings were frequent. Starting from a scattershot

(Continued on page 111)

Right: Justin Murray's toothy take on the new creature.

Below: Using Alien and Predator skins and pieces leftover from *AVP*, Alec Gillis and Steve Koch did some literal cutting and pasting, along with some digital finessing, to come up with this version.

Above: Chris Ayers digitally altered and painted a Steve Wang maquette to explore the PredAlien's coloration.

Left: Another view of Jordu Schell's PredAlien maquette. This shows a fleshier, meatier creature than what ultimately appeared on screen.

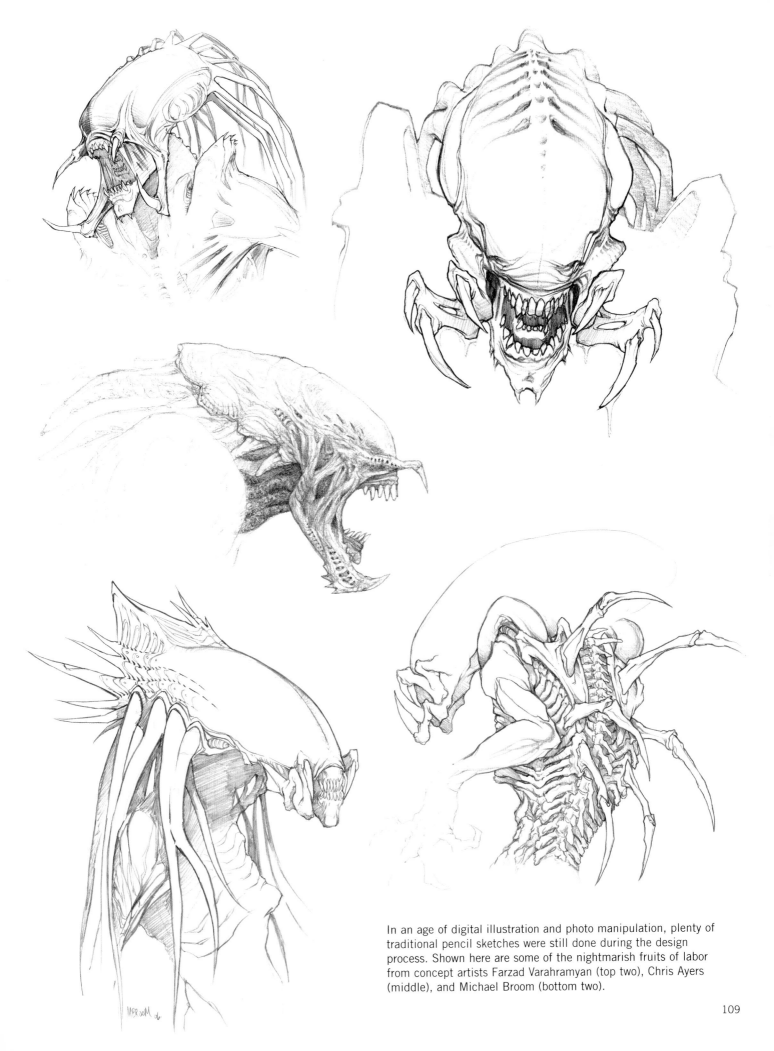

In an age of digital illustration and photo manipulation, plenty of traditional pencil sketches were still done during the design process. Shown here are some of the nightmarish fruits of labor from concept artists Farzad Varahramyan (top two), Chris Ayers (middle), and Michael Broom (bottom two).

109

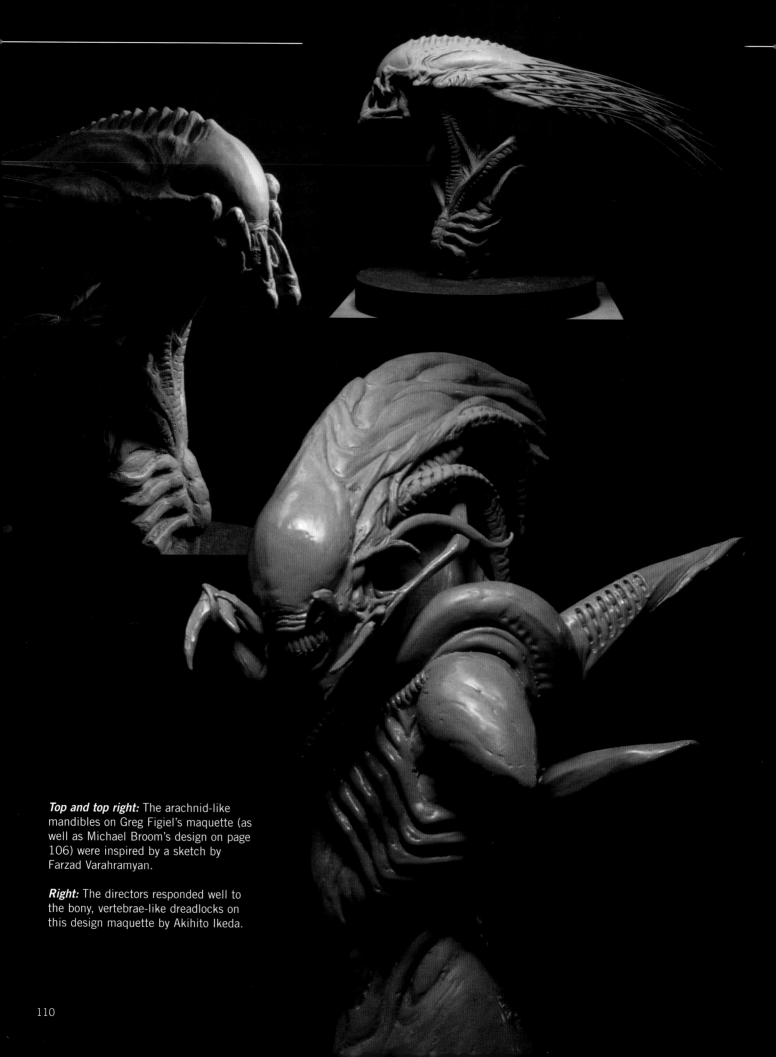

Top and top right: The arachnid-like mandibles on Greg Figiel's maquette (as well as Michael Broom's design on page 106) were inspired by a sketch by Farzad Varahramyan.

Right: The directors responded well to the bony, vertebrae-like dreadlocks on this design maquette by Akihito Ikeda.

(Continued from page 107)

round of drawings we were able to reduce the concepts down to a series of maquettes. After feedback from the directors and the studio, we boiled down the notes into a single maquette sculpted by veteran Steve Wang. He and our team of other sculptors worked furiously on the full-scale sculpture. Artist Chris Ayers produced paint schemes for further comment and eventual approval. A few more design changes were requested while we were sculpting the full-scale creature, and thankfully producer Paul Deason pushed the appearance of the PredAlien to late in the schedule to give us desperately needed time.

The Strauses' desire to make the PredAlien 80 percent Alien and 20 percent Predator was on track, but that begged the question of how this hybrid's behavior would change. A less bestial, more upright posture gives the PredAlien a regal air, and at a few inches taller than the Predator,

Clockwise from top: Maquettes by Steve Wang, Cory Schubert, and Steve Wang. The one to the left features mouth appendages inspired by Alien Facehuggers.

111

it's a more formidable foe. It is also the alpha Alien; the unspoken but inarguable "top dog" that causes other Aliens to cower submissively. The script called for a new form of procreation as well. Regurgitating embryonic Chestbursters down its victim's throat is a bizarre twist on the lifecycle, perhaps a random side effect of the Predator's DNA. Like a ghoulish version of a mother bird feeding its young, the process also makes the PredAlien's mandibles useful for holding the victim's head still. The offspring of the Pred-Alien, having gestated in a human, lose all residual traits of a Predator.

Hopefully the idea of an ever-changing xeno-morph, long accepted in Alien toys and comics, will establish itself firmly in the movie mythos. If so, we may see future installments populated by descendants of science fiction's royal bloodline.

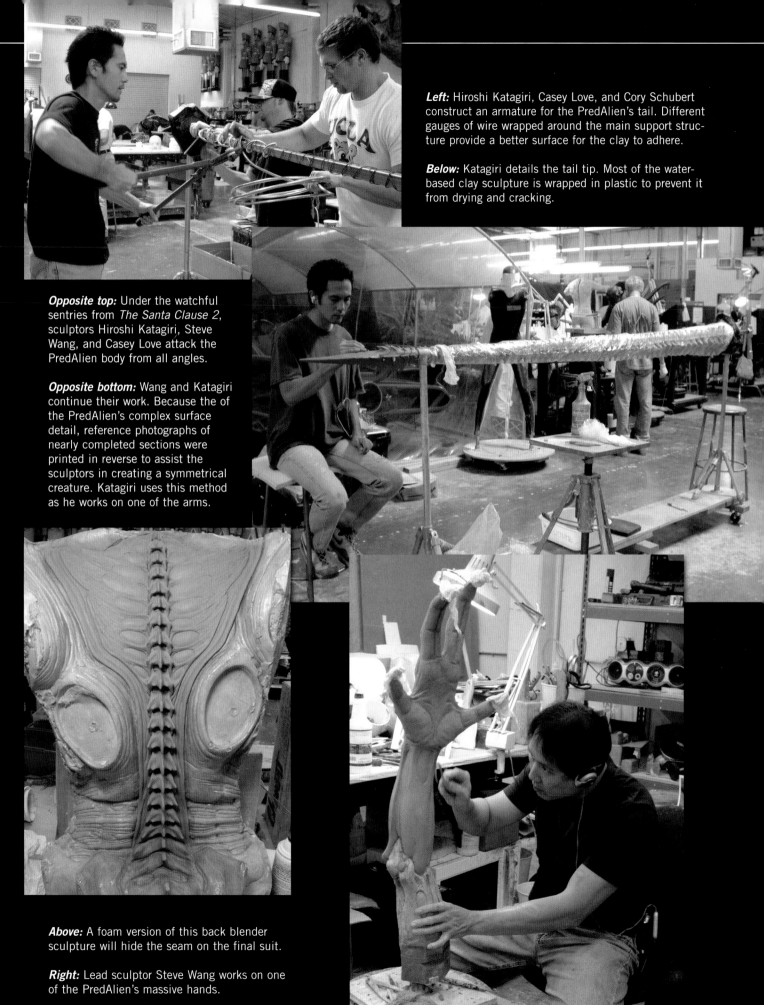

Left: Hiroshi Katagiri, Casey Love, and Cory Schubert construct an armature for the PredAlien's tail. Different gauges of wire wrapped around the main support structure provide a better surface for the clay to adhere.

Below: Katagiri details the tail tip. Most of the water-based clay sculpture is wrapped in plastic to prevent it from drying and cracking.

Opposite top: Under the watchful sentries from *The Santa Clause 2*, sculptors Hiroshi Katagiri, Steve Wang, and Casey Love attack the PredAlien body from all angles.

Opposite bottom: Wang and Katagiri continue their work. Because the of the PredAlien's complex surface detail, reference photographs of nearly completed sections were printed in reverse to assist the sculptors in creating a symmetrical creature. Katagiri uses this method as he works on one of the arms.

Above: A foam version of this back blender sculpture will hide the seam on the final suit.

Right: Lead sculptor Steve Wang works on one of the PredAlien's massive hands.

113

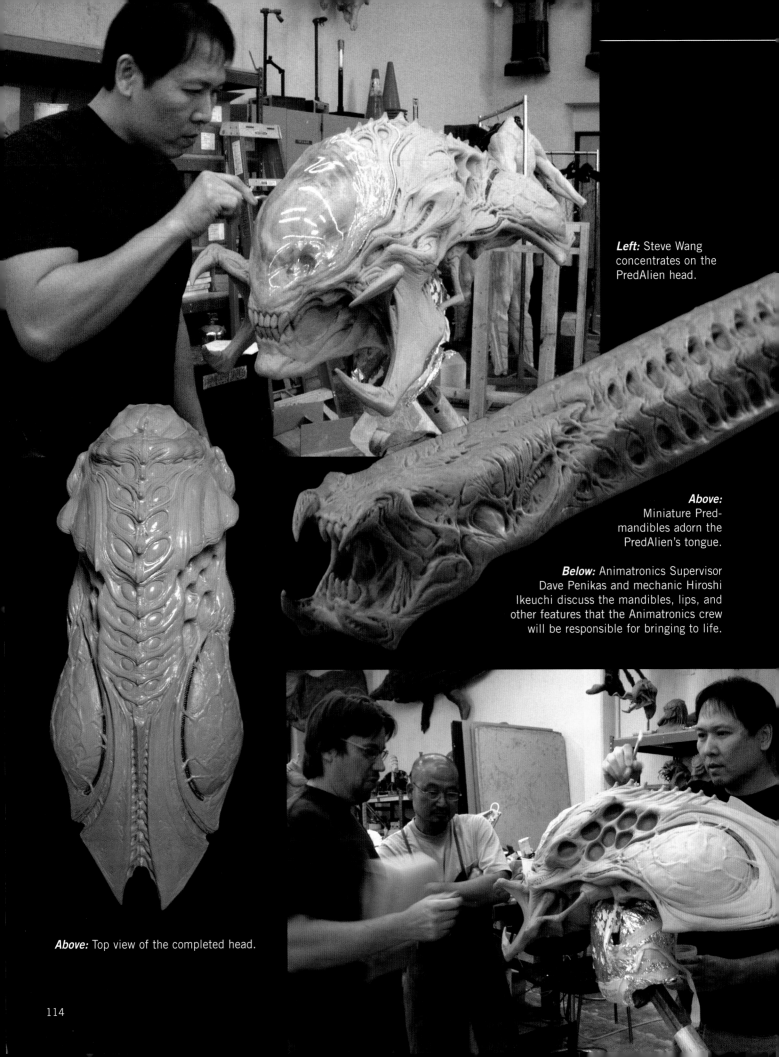

Left: Steve Wang concentrates on the PredAlien head.

Above: Miniature Pred-mandibles adorn the PredAlien's tongue.

Below: Animatronics Supervisor Dave Penikas and mechanic Hiroshi Ikeuchi discuss the mandibles, lips, and other features that the Animatronics crew will be responsible for bringing to life.

Above: Top view of the completed head.

Left: A close-up of the skull beneath the PredAlien's dome.

Below: A blending of Predator and Alien forms and textures comprise the PredAlien torso.

Above: The underside of the creature's head.

Below: Casey Love puts the finishing touches on two of the PredAlien's back pipes.

Below: Jim McLoughlin builds up a clay wall around the head during the molding phase.

Above: Johnnie Saiko Espiritu, Steve Munson, and James Spinner work on the mold of the PredAlien body.

Above: Horacio Fernandez carves registration keys along the arm of the PredAlien, which will ensure the mold locks together and aligns correctly.

Left: A PredAlien hand in the process of being molded.

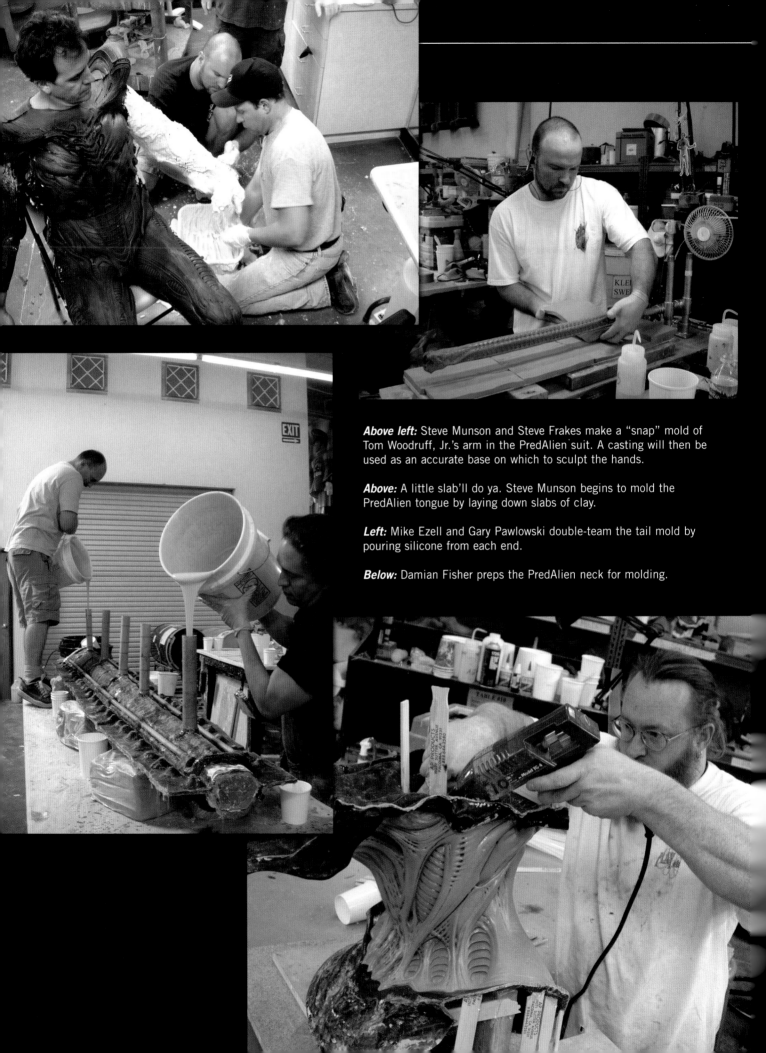

Above left: Steve Munson and Steve Frakes make a "snap" mold of Tom Woodruff, Jr.'s arm in the PredAlien suit. A casting will then be used as an accurate base on which to sculpt the hands.

Above: A little slab'll do ya. Steve Munson begins to mold the PredAlien tongue by laying down slabs of clay.

Left: Mike Ezell and Gary Pawlowski double-team the tail mold by pouring silicone from each end.

Below: Damian Fisher preps the PredAlien neck for molding.

Clockwise from top left: Spencer Whynaucht with the mechanical "skeleton" of "Chet," the full-body Animatronic PredAlien hydraulic puppet. **//** The exposed mechanics of the hero Animatronic PredAlien head to be worn by Tom Woodruff, Jr. **//** "Chet" leans into Rob Derry for an adjustment to his neck. While the PredAlien head was still being sculpted, a Warrior head was temporarily used in its place. **//** Hydraulics Supervisor Marc Irvin delves inside the head mechanisms and controls.

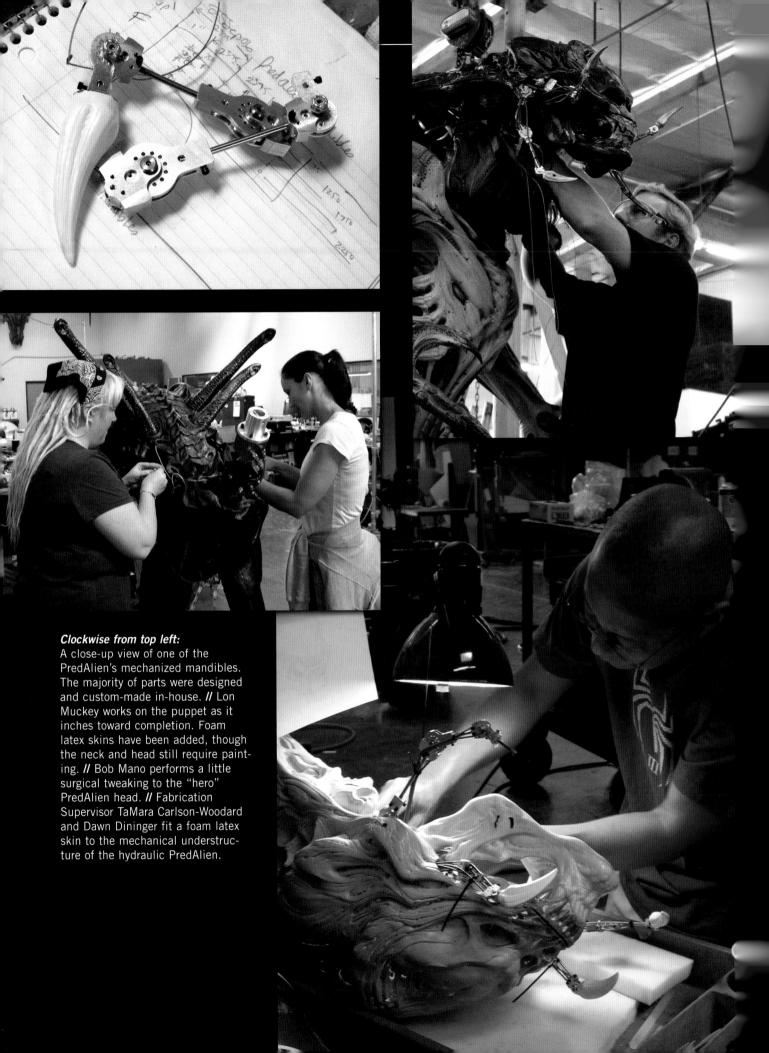

Clockwise from top left:
A close-up view of one of the PredAlien's mechanized mandibles. The majority of parts were designed and custom-made in-house. // Lon Muckey works on the puppet as it inches toward completion. Foam latex skins have been added, though the neck and head still require painting. // Bob Mano performs a little surgical tweaking to the "hero" PredAlien head. // Fabrication Supervisor TaMara Carlson-Woodard and Dawn Dininger fit a foam latex skin to the mechanical understructure of the hydraulic PredAlien.

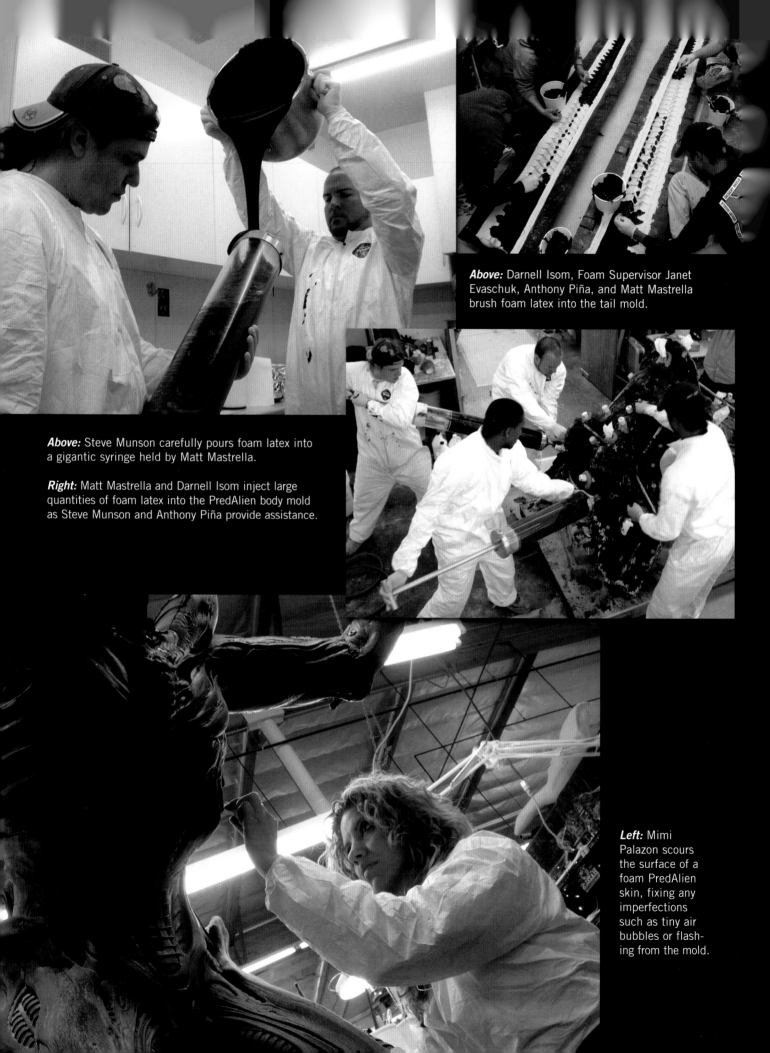

Above: Darnell Isom, Foam Supervisor Janet Evaschuk, Anthony Piña, and Matt Mastrella brush foam latex into the tail mold.

Above: Steve Munson carefully pours foam latex into a gigantic syringe held by Matt Mastrella.

Right: Matt Mastrella and Darnell Isom inject large quantities of foam latex into the PredAlien body mold as Steve Munson and Anthony Piña provide assistance.

Left: Mimi Palazon scours the surface of a foam PredAlien skin, fixing any imperfections such as tiny air bubbles or flashing from the mold.

Below: Probably a little fiercer than a tiger, Finishing Supervisor Tim Leach has a PredAlien by the tail as he checks to make sure the pieces fit and align correctly.

Above: Dawn Dininger and Penny Jane Mackie attach semi-rigid boning to a spandex suit which will be put over the hydraulic PredAlien puppet's mechanical skeleton—and under its foam skin—to give it correct anatomical structure.

Below: Before hard resin claws are added, Penny Jane Mackie affixes snap closures to a pair of PredAlien hands.

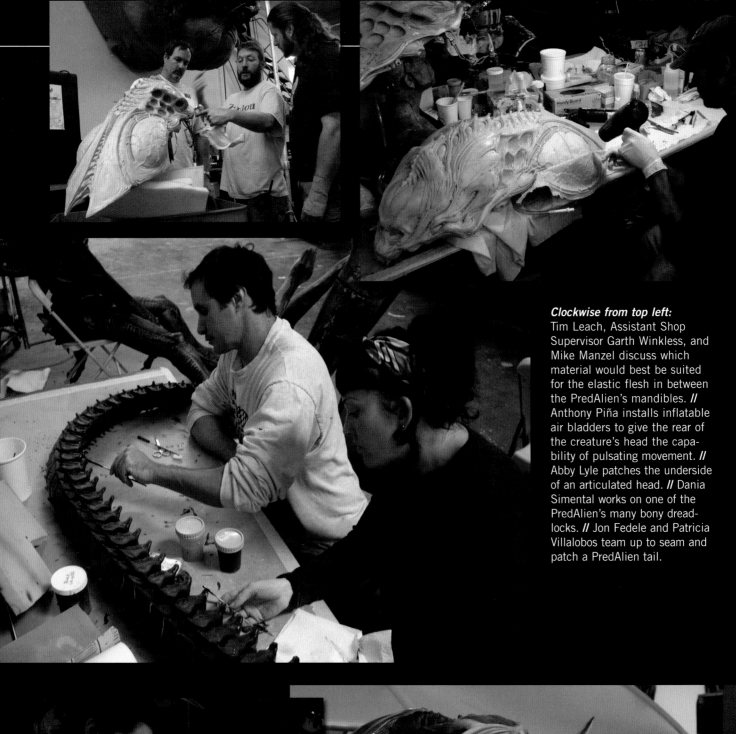

Clockwise from top left:
Tim Leach, Assistant Shop Supervisor Garth Winkless, and Mike Manzel discuss which material would best be suited for the elastic flesh in between the PredAlien's mandibles. **//** Anthony Piña installs inflatable air bladders to give the rear of the creature's head the capability of pulsating movement. **//** Abby Lyle patches the underside of an articulated head. **//** Dania Simental works on one of the PredAlien's many bony dreadlocks. **//** Jon Fedele and Patricia Villalobos team up to seam and patch a PredAlien tail.

Left and below: Paint Supervisor Mike Larrabee rescues the PredAlien from a monochromatic existence.

Below: Koji Ohmura stretches to paint all ten spiky feet of the PredAlien tail.

ALIENS vs. PREDATOR: REQUIEM
Creature Effects by Amalgamated Dynamics, Inc.

Shop Supervisor
Yuri Everson

Assistant Shop Supervisor
Garth Winkless

Mold Shop Supervisor
Steve Frakes

Animatronics Supervisor
Dave Penikas

Lead Sculptors
Steve Wang
Joey Orosco

Hydraulics Supervisor
Marc Irvin

Paint Supervisor
Mike Larrabee

Finishing Supervisor
Tim Leach

Model Shop Supervisor
Nicholas Seldon

Foam Supervisor
Janet Evaschuk

Fabrication Supervisor
TaMara Carlson-Woodard

Concept Artists
Chris Ayers
Thomas Baxa
Michael Broom
Carlos Huante
Chris Howe
Akihito Ikeda
Justin Murray
Jordu Schell
Farzad Varahramyan

Sculptors
Chris Carey
Davis Fandiño
Greg Figiel
Hiroshi Katagiri
Casey Love

Mark Maitre
Michael O'Brien
Cory Schubert
Tully Summers

Model Makers
Tim Arp
Bruce Mitchell

Painters
Brian Clawson
Koji Ohmura

Animatronics Crew
Matthew Borgatti
David Covarrubias
Rob Derry
Rick Galinson
Richard Haugen
Hiroshi Ikeuchi
Robert Mano
Lon Muckey
Brian Namanny
Spencer Whynaucht
Chris Wolters

Animatronic Eye Fabrication
David Hoehn

Electronics Designer
Don Schafer

Mold Makers
David Brooke
Carl Crandall, Jr.
Anthony Diaz
Johnnie Saiko Espiritu
Horacio Fernandez
Damian Fisher
Anthony Grow
Louis Kiss
Mike Ezell
Jim McLoughlin
Steve Munson
Gary Pawlowski
James Spinner
Brian Van Dorn
David Woodruff
Taylor Woodruff

Fabricators
Dawn Dininger
Consuelo Duran
Naomi Gathmann
Penny Jane Mackie
Kristen Willet

Foam Runners
Darnell Isom
Matt Mastrella
Anthony Piña

Finishing
Suma Abuzaineh
Sherry Angelo
Jon Fedele
Matt Killen
Johnathon Killen
Abby Lyle
Mike Manzel
Kevin McTurk
Mimi Palazon
Dania Simental
Patricia Villalobos
Chris Walker

Production Coordinator
Michael Heintzelman

Purchaser
Colin Gillis

Runners
Matthew Sheehan
Pat Todd

Puppeteers
Adam Behr
Jeny Cassady
Morris Chapdelaine
Yuri Everson
Mike Fields
Steve Frakes
George Grove
Paul Hooson
Hiroshi Ikeuchi
Marc Irvin
Frank Meschkuleit
Dave Penikas
Geoff Redknapp
Garth Winkless

On-Set Creature Workshop Leads
Mike Fields
Maiko Gomyo

On-Set Creature Workshop
Adrian Burnett
Charlie Grant
Gideon Hay
J.P. Mass

On-Set Special Skills Costumers
Scott Blackie
Summer Eves
Valerie Fawkes-Kim
Tatiana Hutenic
Maya Mani
Sam McKinnon
Mary Wiseman

On-Set Breakdown Artists
Karen Durant
Charis Tillson

WEAR EYE
PROTECTION
WHEN BUSTING
STUFF UP

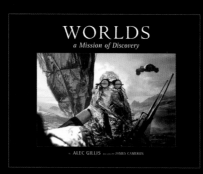

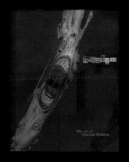

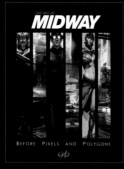

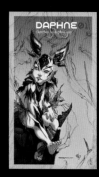